THE **9** TRAITS OF
HERO BRANDS

THE NINE TRAITS OF
HERO BRANDS

International Business Leader
HESHAM
ALMEKKAWI

Interior book design and editing by Mike Lewis - USA
Cover book design by TeamD

Table of Contents

Acknowledgments

There are special people in our lives that pave the way for us and make it possible for us to go the extra mile.

To My lovely wife, Cress, who has supported me for the last twenty-one years.

To my wonderful kids, Howayda, Ziad, Rami and Marwan, who light up my life every day.

To John Maxwell for encouraging me to add value every day.

To Mike Lewis for his help in designing and editing this book.

To everyone I have worked with and taught me something along the way.

And to my teams over the years, who supported me and believed in our journeys. You have made me a better person and a better leader.

Thank You!

Introduction

During my career as a manager, executive, and college professor, brands have appeared and faded into history, many little noticed before they collapsed. I have managed branding programs that created long-lasting values and others that failed to move potential customers. "Why do some brands save companies and others are expensive disasters?" I wondered. Brands that survive difficult periods, exceed expectations, and lead to growing profits deserve the title of "Hero Brands."

This book is for those seeking to increase revenues, extend your company's image, or improve its reputation. Brands – the alter egos of the companies they represent - are universal across multiple industries and the focus of this book.

Companies spend years building brand equity. It takes time to develop a dominant culture that becomes the basis of a company brand. Working with franchisors and in the Food and Beverage (F&B) industry, I realized the differences between brands that excelled and those that struggled. I learned Hero Brands share nine common traits that are missing in the brands of companies with mediocre or poor performance. The traits, purposely developed by company management, separate the excellent companies from the also-rans.

What is a brand?

A "brand" is the intangible image of an organization in the minds of the public or consumers. Companies can influence how consumers view a brand, reinforce it by developing an organizational culture that supports it, and aggressively promote it. Nevertheless, customers ultimately define a brand.

The essence of a brand is the customer's perception of their relationship with the brand. They want to know what makes an underlying business unique and how its products relate to them. Most of all, consumers want to know if they can trust a brand to deliver on its promises. Is the brand a carefully designed collection of exaggerated promises and advertising hype? Does the brand accurately reflect the internal culture of the business? A successful brand, a Hero brand, "walks the talk."

A connection between a brand and its customers generates long-term, persistent loyalty. Consider the Hero brands of Coke and Pepsi. A Coke consumer rarely drinks a Pepsi soda, given a choice, and vice versa. The product's taste is secondary to the consumer's feelings for the brand, as many taste tests prove.

Successful brands forge an almost unbreakable bond with consumers. Loyalty and a solid brand link across products, industries, and geography. The bond generally extends to a company's new products or expansion into new geographical territories. For example, those who own a Nissan Altima are more likely to purchase another Nissan model than a Toyota with similar features. Nissan has earned their trust by consistently meeting the expectations of its customers, i.e., delivering on its implied promises in the past.

Why should you care?

Most people prefer companies with good brands, but only some understand how a good brand becomes exceptional. Hero brands deliver long-term sales growth. Apple, Google, Microsoft, and Starbucks are examples of well-established Hero Brands. During 2012-2021, each company's sales growth was more than double the general market rate.

Hero Brand status has many benefits, including diverting cash flow from marketing to improving customers' experience. The marketing budget for the average S&P 500 company ranged from 6.4% to 9.5% of sales revenues in 2021. By contrast, budgets for Hero brands range from Disney's 3% to Microsoft's 1.1%. Successful brands rely on their customers' promoting the brand, reducing the need for ultra-expensive advertising campaigns.

Hero Brands Growth Rates 2012 - 2021 (in billions)			
	2012	2021	CAGR
Apple	$ 164.69	$ 378.32	8.7%
Google*	$ 46.04	$ 257.64	18.8%
Microsoft	$ 72.93	$ 184.90	9.8%
Starbucks	$ 13.63	$ 30.36	8.3%
S&P 500	$1,092.37	$1,566.80	3.7%

*Alphabet

Financial indicators – return on investment (ROI), positive cash flow, lower employee turnover, and recruitment costs – generally favor Hero brand companies. Employees are more engaged, working in positive cultures focused on customers and their experience with the business. Raising capital is easier when a brand has an excellent reputation and credibility.

Engaged, connected customers elevate the brand. They help grow and protect the brand, propelling a good brand into a Hero Brand that lasts generations.

What defines a HERO Brand?

Only a select few meet the standards of a Hero Brand. Heroes are an exclusive group that constantly exhibits the nine traits I identify in this book. Some may debate my choices, adding, deleting, or redefining one or more to fit their experience. My list of traits is not exclusive or complete. However, they result from years of working with multiple brands and studying others.

My analysis is a summation of the traits I have personally witnessed. I do not claim to be the only source of knowledge, nor that my journey to learn the requirements of a superior brand is complete. I do hope readers will find my observations and suggestions thoughtful and thought-provoking as they seek to explore the powerful benefits of branding.

Trait 1: Fill a Market in the Gap

Brands often fail because company management does not identify or understand the nuances of their brand and the targeted customer base. Whether your business competes in an existing market, or you expect to develop a new one, a clear understanding of your objectives and the needs of your targeted consumers is imperative.

A market gap is a space where a significant unfilled customer need exists or the existing competitors' offerings, and customer needs misalign. Gaps are opportunities to grow your customer base and protect your competitive position. Brand positioning in a new market requires a different strategy (**Be first**) than entering an existing or mature market (**Be better**).

Understanding Your Brand

Exploiting a brand is only possible by knowing your potential customers' feelings about it. Executives are fond of being told what they want to hear, an unfortunate tendency like drinking your bathwater. Success breeds hubris and exaggerated confidence in the power of a brand. Customer needs constantly change. Consequently, **no brand can meet all customers' needs for every product at all times and circumstances.**

An organization and its brand are like chefs and their meals. The chef buys the freshest ingredients, carefully measures the quantities, adds the secret spices, and lovingly stirs the pot. Servers dressed in formal tuxedos deliver the steaming dish to the table with great flair, carefully positioned on the finest China plate, a feast for the senses. Despite the chef's effort, care, and expense to produce an exquisite dining experience, the diner is the only judge of the meal's success. Companies, like chefs, influence a customer's perception, but the brand's value is only in the customer's mind.

Misunderstanding and misusing a brand confuses consumers and usually ends badly.

- Colgate® is one of America's best-known brands, one of the first companies to sell toothpaste in a jar, then a collapsible tube. Giddy with their market success, the company entered the frozen meal market with Colgate® Kitchen Entrees in 1982. The brand extension failed as consumers connected the meals to a toothpaste taste. The market could not accept the premise that a company making toothpaste would also excel in producing tasty food. The ill-fated venture also caused toothpaste sales to drop.

- Frito-Lay, the unquestioned giant of snack foods, apparently missed the Colgate® gaffe. Or they thought a food company's brand could be successful in cosmetics. In 2005, the company launched

Cheetos' flavored lip balm in a bright orange tube. Cheetos lovers and other consumers avoided the product in droves, forcing its recall within months and causing red faces at the company headquarters.

Branding is neither art nor science but a combination of both. The only way to determine the success of a branding effort is through ongoing formal and informal consumer research using multiple tools and techniques, including personal interviews, surveys, and independent company/product reviews. A company's financial statements indirectly measure customer satisfaction by sales growth by product, average ticket size, product returns, and repeat customers. Website analytics are typically available at little cost.

Brands and consumers exist in a constantly evolving ecosystem. Technology and social change weaken a brand's power over time, misaligning the brand's promise and customer expectations. For example, a broad network of brick-and-mortar locations is a liability when consumers prefer online shopping.

It is crucial to identify a difference between the company's perception of its brand and how consumers view the same brand. Companies must nourish brands to remain effective. When differences appear, company management can respond by improving problem areas to meet consumer expectations (rehabilitation), adjusting their business objectives to reflect the consumer's feelings about the brand (reinforcement), or rebranding the company to clean the slate (restart).

Whatever the findings of brand research, knowing how customers perceive a brand is mandatory before attempting to expand into gaps in a market.

Finding the Gap

I'm often asked, "How can I recognize a market in the gap?" The simple and correct answer is "Ask the customer." Company management sometimes begin market planning to find a market for a product, not vice versa. Their approach is like having a round cylinder and trying to find a round hole where it fits. Identifying a customer's need first, then seeking a solution, is usually the better and least expensive approach.

Dean Kamen, the inventor of the Segway, was enamored with the technical achievements behind his two-wheeled, self-balancing scooter. For more than a year, the invention was subject to a global marketing campaign about the "most revolutionary product since the computer." At its launch on Good Morning America's television show, its inventor promised it would transform mobile transportation. After spending millions of dollars, the company discovered that most people were happy with walking and did not need an impractical, expensive, complicated machine. Aside from mall cops and the occasional tour guide, no one purchased the Segway. It remains the perfect example of beginning a business with a customer, not a product.

Tools to Identify Market Gaps

Many companies, especially startups, fail to do the market research necessary to identify specific customer needs and ways to target those consumers with unmet needs. Fortunately, multiple tools are available to identify market gaps and how your existing brand might fill the void.

PEST Analysis

While included in this section of analytical tools about market gaps, PEST analysis is a tool to understand the general market for your brand better, whether in your current or new markets. PEST stands for the broad, economy-wide influences of **P**olitics, **E**conomics, **S**ociety, and **T**echnology that affect businesses and communities on a large scale. Some analysts expand the analysis by including laws and regulations and the environment as influences (a PESTLE analysis).

A PESTLE analysis is a macro-view of a market. Its output enables organizations and individuals to identify change as early as possible and capitalize on it. It also recognizes potential and active threats so you can proactively avoid or mitigate them. The analysis typically requires research to accurately identify and verify the broad changes likely to affect the business ecosystem. A sample of PESTLE questions include:

- **Politics:** When is the next election? What is the possibility of a change of power? How could a change impact the regulatory environment of your brand? When would these changes occur?

- **Economy**: What is the trend of future GDP levels? What are the expectations of inflation? What is the unemployment rate? How will the Central Bank affect interest rates? How stable is the economy? What trends in consumer buying power might impact your brand negatively or positively?

- **Society**: What demographic changes will affect your customer base? Are there any religious or cultural drivers that might affect your brand? Has there been a shift in customers' behavior or work patterns that could impact your brand?

- **Technology**: Will emerging technologies affect your brand? If so, how? Is the competition developing or buying new technology that could change the direction of the market?

- **Law and regulations**. Are regulations affecting your business changing? Is enforcement of regulations more aggressive or lenient? How will potential tax law changes affect the financial health of your business?

- **Environment**. How does climate change affect your operations? How does it affect your current and potential customers? What environmental regulations are likely? Are the regulations opportunities or threats?

A PEST analysis affects a brand by confirming or challenging the outlook for the company behind the brand. Consequently, companies might discontinue, defer, alter, or advance plans to enter or protect existing markets.

SWOT Analysis

SWOT analyses help align your brand with your customers' needs and identify those qualities that create a competitive advantage for your products in the minds of your targeted customers. The analysis covers your brand's **S**trengths, **W**eaknesses, **O**pportunities, and **T**hreats. SWOT analyses also helps identify vulnerabilities in your brand that your competitors can exploit.

A SWOT analysis requires answering a series of questions, based on consumer research, about your brand. Whether moving into an unoccupied market gap or entering an existing market targeting unmet needs, the analysis prepares you offensively (moving into the market) and defensively (protecting any gains you secure).

Markets – virgin and mature – are the battlefields of brands. Over-estimating your strengths or under-estimating your weaknesses can lead to failure, a diminishment of the brand, and lost investment.

Sun Tzu, an ancient Chinese General, is credited with the book *The Art of War*, an influential work on military strategy. His advice that "He will win who knows when to fight and when not to fight" is as relevant to business competitions as to national wars.

BRAND SWOT ANALYSIS

STRENGTHS	OPPORTUNITIES
• Why do customers prefer your products? • What are the advantages of your brand? • How is your brand better than your competitors?	• What market segments are overlooked? • Where are your competitors most vulnerable? • What market trends favor your products?
WEAKNESSES	**THREATS**
• What are your customers' major complaints? • How are competitors superior to you? • What aspects of your brand fail to resonate with your customers?	• What are the market advantages of competitors? • Does technology advances affect your products? • Are your competitors better financed?

A SWOT analysis is not a silver bullet but a snapshot of your brand, the status of the competition, and the advantages your brand can exploit. The insight gained from the analysis validates the likelihood of success. It identifies areas where your brand can outperform the competition.

Market Mapping/Perceptual Mapping

Market mapping identifies market gaps with opportunities favoring a brand. A market map illustrates gaps in a market along two dimensions of choice. A typical market map compares quality and price along two axes. Areas with no or few points indicate potential gaps in the market. Similarly, an area with multiple points suggests an established marketplace with fierce rivalry. The market map for rated hotels in Riyadh, Saudi Arabia, suggests a potential market for lower-priced hotels for cost-conscious travelers.

**MARKET MAP OF RATED HOTELS
IN RIYADH, SAUDI ARABIA**

High Price

★★★★★
(21)

★★★★
(24)

Low   ★★★   High
Density   (34)   Density

★★
(5)

Low Price

When I discussed the importance of the right product for a market with a group of Middle Eastern young entrepreneurs in Dubai, a young person from Saudi Arabia summed up the lesson: "Don't try to sell Jet Skis in Riyadh." I could not have said it better!

The lack of competition in the lower price range does not automatically mean there is a market within the gap but an area that needs further study. When I worked for Americana Group in the late 2000s, a market map showed no Mexican fast-food places in Dubai. Since the F&B industry had been growing exponentially for years, the lack of a restaurant serving popular ethnic food seemed a great opportunity. Taco Bell has been a success in the U.S. for years. Logically, it should do well in the Middle East. We had high expectations based on the brand's performance in the United States and international markets.

I was responsible for opening three Taco Bell establishments in 2009 and 2010, each opening with massive publicity and excitement. Shortly after we opened the last restaurant, we realized our research was incomplete. While Taco Bell appeared to fill the gap for Mexican food in the region, customers viewed Taco Bell meals as snacks with little value for the money. We could not afford to sell a taco for a U.S. price of $1 since we were importing most of the raw materials from abroad. The three units closed after two years and huge losses. Other Mexican brands subsequently withdrew from the market for the same reasons.

What looked like a great opportunity was a massive disappointment because there was no market in the gap. In retrospect, we tried to create a customer for the product instead of a product for the customer. It is never about what the CEO or the executives think will work; it is about what the customer needs—knowingly or unknowingly. To succeed, companies must create a product to fulfill known needs or create a demand for an unknown product.

A market map provides insight into a market, but it alone is insufficient to justify a move in the gap. Further examination is needed, especially to questions like "Why does the gap exist?" and "Why haven't competitors entered that market? Asking what they know may be something you do not know. Being cautious can save money, resources, and reputation in the long run.

Gaps in Different Market Conditions

Two of the most common competition scenarios are the pioneer and mature markets. ***Be first or be better.*** Pioneer brands focus on unfilled needs. The most successful pioneers choose markets that are difficult for competition to enter, then attempt to build barriers to keep competitors out.

Pioneer Brands

Being first in a market has advantages if the brand delivers on its promises and moves quickly and decisively to protect its position. The first-mover advantage can only carry a brand so far because lucrative markets attract competitors like bees to honey. Being first to fill the gap is not enough; a brand must maintain its leadership position.

- Xerox invented mechanical copying, obsoleting carbon papers to the gratitude of all secretaries. The brand became so dominant that "Xerox" became synonymous with making a copy on any device, regardless of the brand. Using its copier as a springboard, the company subsequently introduced word processing machines, printers, an office communications network (Ethernet), and "erasable paper."

- Kleenex tissue paper is an example of an older product rebranded to fill a market gap. The product initially developed during WWI as a gas mask filter was initially repositioned as "Kotex" in the mid-1920s. With a slight change in its competition, the material was subsequently branded "Kleenex" and marketed as a woman's cold cream and makeup remover. Kimberly-Clark, the tissue manufacturer, continues to expand its use, becoming so ubiquitous that the word "Kleenex" to any facial tissue. The phrase "grab a Kleenex" is commonplace.

- Dell Computers is an excellent example of a pioneering brand that recognized a market for custom computers, each designed to fit a particular customer's choices. They then leveraged their reputation for quality products and service, including mass-produced computers available online with quick delivery times.

Many companies have used first-mover advantages to create a Hero brand where the brand is synonymous with the task it represents. The list includes Google, Zipper, FedEx, and Bubble wrap. Each brand became a market leader, making it difficult for competitors to follow.

Ironically, there are more examples of company brands with pioneer status that failed than successes. Walkman pioneered the portable music market, relying on older technology but could not upgrade to newer electronic formats. Apple found the niche of mobile music with its iPod and has never looked back.

MySpace was once the social media leader, and E-Toys.com pioneered online toy sales. Both companies disrupted whole industries by accurately projecting changing customer needs for their services. However, neither company secured its first-mover advantage, allowing competitors to enter their space and take market share. Successful brands fill gaps in markets. Hero Brands fill a gap, then becomes the dominant competitor.

Mature Market Brands

Mature markets tend to have fierce competition with lesser growth. Every pioneer market matures as competitors seek to reap the bounty uncovered by the pioneers.

Differentiators are critical in a mature market. Hero Brands entering mature markets improve the value proposition to gain market share. They use their brands to lure customers with features of convenience, availability, better customer service, quicker deliveries, and other benefits honed and embedded into their DNA. They capitalize on oversaturated markets where their brand can dominate, forcing competitors to fail or leave the market.

Amazon is an excellent example of a Hero Brand in a mature market. When their growth stalled in online shopping, they increased their innovation efforts, analyzing each market for improvements and the next evolution of need. They introduced "Dash" buttons, small physical stickers that automatically reordered specific merchandise when pushed. Though the experiment failed to meet expectations (a typical home required over 500 buttons), it led to new delivery improvements like the ongoing trials to use robotic drones for package deliveries.

Customers only flock to a brand if that brand offers something different, unique, and relevant. McDonald's is a prime example of a Hero Brand that routinely enters a market late. Waiting for the right time and the right location is McDonald's strategy. Several years ago, I opened two small restaurants, KFC and Hardee's, in a remote area in the United Arab Emirates (UAE). Three years after we opened and established a profitable market, Mickey D' moved in with two flagship locations within meters of our places.

The McDonald's facilities were quadruple the size of our restaurants combined and featured play areas and drive-throughs. They marketed a total restaurant experience close to our restaurants to capture our customers.

Being a Hero brand is more than quickly filling a gap or meeting customer expectations. Their mission is to be the best and last the longest.

Hero Brand Tips

Hero Brands seek controlled growth, coordinating the elements of finance, operations, and marketing to establish consistent profits and market leadership. Explosive growth is not controlled and can lead to a collapse even when the brand is performing at its best. Hero Brands stay ahead of the curve and continually leads the market. They practice the agility to react proactively to surprises, especially customer needs trends.

When I lived in New York City in the mid-1980s, Blockbuster was the unquestioned leader of the home video rental industry. They aggressively transitioned from VHS tape to DVD to Blu-Ray without a major hiccup. The company introduced a monthly unlimited in-store rental subscription program, then extended it to include a hybrid system of in-store and mail rentals.

The future seemed bright, perhaps so promising that the company missed new competitors that irrevocably changed the industry. Netflix initially offered a mail rental program and expanded to on-demand video streaming. Redbox eliminated the need for expensive inventory, focusing on the most popular rentals, and expensive brick-and-mortar locations by setting up vending machines in high-traffic areas. Today, one Blockbuster store remains a nostalgic reminder of how people viewed movies once upon a time.

What went wrong with Blockbuster? Their downfall was their failure to recognize how technological and social change would affect their business. Given the opportunity to acquire Netflix in its early days, they could not see the future and the effects of video streaming on physical video rentals. Blockbuster should have recognized the difference in convenience between ordering a Netflix movie streamed over the television and driving from home to a store to rent or return a movie. Creating a product to fulfill the need for greater convenience led to the Netflix brand.

Hero Brands actively research and continually position for the future. They understand that a product must have a market to succeed. The right timing is essential, as early or late introduces unnecessary problems.

Summary

Hero Brands discover the right differentiators to become household names. The differentiators may be features, functionality, brand image, service, convenience, price, quality, or other brand qualities. They expand their vision horizontally to related markets while maintaining consistency moving forward. They protect the brand's identity, no matter what happens.

Heroes identify market gaps and thoroughly investigate their history and parameters to ensure a viable market before committing. Hero Brands have the momentum necessary for future sustainability. They use any tools available to make informed and strategic decisions. Do your homework and make sure that the timing is right. Create a product for the demand or create a need for a product, but never create a customer for a product.

Trait 2: Experiential with Defined Personality

Appearance initially attracts us to someone, but their personality determines the length of the relationship. Appearances can be deceiving, and the truth behind the idiom "never judge a book by its cover." Personality is the intangible combination of thoughts, feelings, and behavior that makes each person unique.

Brands have personalities, too. Consider the differences between your feelings about Apple and IBM. Both make computers with a wide range of features and prices. Most IT experts consider their performance similar. Even so, each company has created a brand personality that appeals to a particular customer type. According to consumer surveys, the companies are viewed very differently in the marketplace:

- The Apple personality is inventive, fun, and empowering. The company boosts its image with bright colors, futuristic designs, and pictures of happy young people using iPhones and iPads in social groups or the Super Bowl XVIII advertisement introducing the Macintosh in 1984. Some have characterized the brand personality as Dory, the slightly goofy regal blue tang fish in Disney movies.

• IBM's personality is very different from Apple's brand, triggering feelings of reliability, efficiency, and competence. Its products favor traditional designs and muted colors, and its ads feature business function competence. The personification of IBM is that of a conservative country banker in a three-piece suit.

Personalities are the traits that connect you to a brand. The emotional connection does not require the actual use of a product. A friend's recommendation, an advertisement that touched you, or a favorite celebrity's endorsement colors your feelings and defines a brand's personality.

A successful brand personality persists for years, remaining influential long after the targeted consumer ages and moves beyond their initial demographic. Several years ago, while walking in a mall with my wife, she noticed a Forever 21 store. She recalled the many times, when she was younger and single, buying her clothes in a similar shop. Spurred by affectionate, nostalgic memories of those experiences, she could not resist the urge to enter the store to see the new styles. I believe that her connection with the brand will last a lifetime.

When you think of a favorite brand, product specifications are probably not at the top of the list. Thoughts of a past enjoyable or successful experience with the brand are more likely. Our past encounters have emotional contexts, good and bad. Research suggests that these emotions, not logic, determine 80% of the decisions we make each day.

Imagine shopping for cereal in your local market. As you walk between the rows of tiered shelves filled with brightly colored boxes, how do you decide which brand to buy? Do you carefully examine each box, reading the ingredients and expiration date? Most shoppers enter a store with the brand they want already in mind, a connection of good experiences with the brand forged over time.

Brand Personality Types

Personality and image are not the same, though both influence feelings about a brand. The latter is about brand attributes or content, including its products' appeal, ease of use, functionality, fame, and overall value. Personality speaks to the brand's character – how the company relates to the consumer. Brand characters range from trustworthy, friendly, exciting, and comfortable to arrogant, focused, innovative, and disruptive.

Companies create brand personalities to build an emotional connection with their targeted customers. Successful relationships bolster brand loyalty resulting in the shopper's purchase of the company's products. Decisions about a brand's personality should be carefully chosen and be:

- **Authentic** – Consumers quickly distinguish between what is real and what is fake. Brand authenticity depends on the alignment of three factors: key brand attributes, management strategies to communicate those attributes, and consumer outcomes with the brand. A brand must be "faithful and true to itself and its consumers, and support consumers being true to themselves."

- **Logical** – The relationship between a brand's personality and its products must be easily understood by the targeted consumer, especially when a company seeks to extend the brand into new categories and markets. Marketing books are full of examples where consumers cannot see the link between a company's personality and its products. Cadbury's, a British-owned confectionary company noted for its fine chocolates, entered the instant food market with Smash, instant mashed potatoes in a can. While the product lingered for years, the connection confused consumers and hurt the perceived quality of its confectionery products.

- **Relatable**. Successful brand personalities touch a responsive chord in the minds of consumers. That connection is the impetus to purchase the product. Research suggests that consumers are more likely to buy a brand if its personality is like theirs. For example, conservative, introverted, older people are more likely to buy a Cadillac Escalade than a Tesla Plaid+ model.

Defining a soft drink brand personality is difficult because each company's products have the same contents: sugar, water, flavoring agents, and carbon dioxide (CO_2). Consequently, the different brands try to create an emotional connection distinct from the product.

When was the last time you heard or saw a TV ad for Coke or Pepsi highlighting the taste? Never! Cola ads aim to portray a particular feeling that relates to their customers. People like to be around energetic, trustworthy, cool people having fun. Brands intend to create the same likable personality traits to become your friend.

There are generally five types of *personalities* typically used with brands:

- *Competence* suggests reliability, intelligence, and success. The brand is considered its industry's thought leader, who reacts carefully and thoughtfully to events and circumstances that affect the industry. The brand personalities of Microsoft, UPS, Blue Cross, and JPMorgan Chase emphasize the quiet competence of industry leaders who are rarely flustered or seduced by high-risk ventures.

- *Excitement* elicits feelings of youth, imagination, freedom, and passion. Brands with this personality are the daring, the rebels, and the adventurers. They are John Travolta's Tony Manero character in *Saturday Night Fever* and Maggie Pollit (Elizabeth Taylor) in Tennessee Williams' *Cat on a Hot Tin Roof*. Companies like Nike, MTV, and Disney attract us with their promise of fun and flair.

- *Sophistication* is the aura of elegance, charm, and class. Brands with these personalities assert their uniqueness and elite status. They appeal to the connoisseur, not the crowd. Brands considered sophisticated include American Express, Rolls Royce, Patek Philippe, and Grey Poupon, refined, prestigious, tasteful, and opulent display traits associated with *sophistication*.

- *Sincerity* is generally associated with honesty, wholesomeness, and kindness. Sincere brands like Campbell Soups, Hallmark, and Pampers are down-to-earth and trigger feelings of nostalgia, family values, and trust. While all brands seek to be sincere, these brands become part of the family, the grandmother who is always there with an open lap and a gentle smile.

- *Ruggedness* in a brand personality promises durability, utility, practicality, and strength. "What you see is what you get" is the message. Companies with outdoor, construction, and sports products like Patagonia, Yeti, Jeep, and Craftsman favor rugged personalities. Advertisements for these brands typically feature images of flannel shirts, campfires, and farms.

Brand Differentiation

Companies use their brand personality to differentiate themselves from their competition. The fast-food chains - McDonald's, Burger King, and Hardees - offer similar products in the same price range but attract customers for different reasons:

- McDonald's arches represent convenience, certainty, and comfort. Customers trust that the menu and food quality will be the same in Dubai, New York and Phoenix, Arizona.

- Burger King's personality suggests quality and customization. They sell food fit for a king, char-broiled over an open flame rather than frying on a greasy griddle. Customers choose their ingredients to fit their taste preferences.

- Hardee's brand features quantity and value with notoriously large portions and plenty of calories. No one walks away hungry after a Hardee's meal.

The three competitors focus on different consumer motivations. Each develops loyal customers by consistently delivering their brand messages and differentiated personalities.

Brand Positioning

Many companies waste their efforts developing their brand's personality because they incorrectly position their brand in the market. Positioning is the process that communicates the brand's personality to the consumer's mind. Positioning influences consumer perceptions and answers the question, "Why should I buy your product?"

"Positioning is not what you do to a product. Positioning is what you do to the mind of the prospect. That is, you position the product in the mind of the prospect.

Positioning is more than messaging, a value proposition, or differentiation. It is the strategic decisions that tell consumers why your product is unique and better than other alternatives. Branding and positioning are mutually dependent. Brands with the wrong positioning are ineffective.

A well-executed brand positioning strategy opens more opportunities to connect with customers. It helps a business stand out from others offering similar products. Successful positioning is powerful. For example, when a child scrapes their knee, do you apply a bandage or a Band-Aid?

Companies use different brand positioning strategies, including:

- **Service-Based.** Companies in industries with poor customer service or complex products that are difficult to operate often highlight their robust support systems to differentiate themselves. Apple advertises its Superior customer service to justify a higher price point. Only those companies that can deliver the promised service should use this strategy since the response to failures is typically exaggerated.

- **Convenience-Based**. A convenience-based strategy emphasizes that a company's products are more available or less complicated to use. Factors like readily accessible, multiple locations, and easy-to-use product designs attract busy consumers anxious to complete their tasks. Consumers are usually willing to pay more for convenience, the reason that a gallon of milk costs more in a convenience store than in a supermarket.

- **Price-Based.** Companies present their products as inexpensive or lower cost in the market. The lowest-cost provider in a market usually captures the highest market share but runs the risk of being considered lower quality with limited applications. Price-based positioning can trigger expensive price wars between competitors.

- **Quality-Based.** Companies using this strategy emphasize the quality of their product through exceptional craftsmanship and high-quality materials. Some companies utilize their "green" products and processes to recognize environmental concerns.

- **Technology-Based.** Consumers who value innovation are attracted to leading-edge products that disrupt industries. The "pushing the envelope" strategy appeals to consumers focused on the future and the promise of breakthrough applications.

There is no perfect brand positioning strategy. All can be successful in the right environment, and all can miss the mark. The goal of creating a brand personality and implementing a positioning strategy is to align both to the targeted consumer group.

The Experiential Factor

Once upon a time, customers looked for the best food, service, products, or price whenever dining or shopping.

Cinemagoers cared more about the movie than the comfort of their seat or the amenities offered by the theater. Customers will always seek the highest perceived value in exchange for their money. However, the definition of "value" has changed in recent years.

Today, consumers value a product or service for its overall experience, not necessarily the product or service's features (or lack thereof). Satisfaction is a holistic outcome, much more than feelings about a single element.

The Disney World Effect

Over 58 million customers visit Disney World each year. Few come for the meals they might eat, the gifts available in the gift shop, or their choice of accommodation. They willingly accept hour-long waits, high prices, and rude fellow visitors to share the experience with others.

Despite the inconveniences, most visitors are happy from when they arrive to their departure, pleased with their memories with family or friends. Heavy rain drenched the park the day my family and I visited. Despite the clouds, the constant dripping, and the wet feet, the visit was fantastic and worth its high price.

Experience-seeking: Opportunity and Threat

Nowadays, the idea of total experience is the norm for customer engagement. For example, phone companies compete on the breadth of their networks, financing plans, and phones with an ever-expanding list of utilities, services, and applications. Consumers expect their phones to be convenient, attractive, reasonably priced, and reliable, with the capabilities of a camera, GPS locator, entertainment, and access to external data sources.

When consumer tastes or expectations change, rebranding or repositioning may appear necessary. Either strategy is challenging to achieve and invariably expensive. The effort will test the credibility and authenticity of the company. Failure nullifies years of effort to establish a trusted position in consumer minds.

Typical Personality and Positioning Mistakes

Companies sometimes lose their way in the hot wars of competition. Over-reach is a constant concern of successful companies. Management needs to recognize the limits of its brand personality or ensure its positioning remains effective in a volatile marketplace. Success is temporary and requires constant market and competitive research to maintain relevancy.

Blockbuster's failure to recognize the impact of on-demand video streaming was fatal. Walmart's faith in its bricks-and-mortar and low prices enabled Amazon to capture a dominant position in online retail. While progress results from learning from failure, the adage that the seeds of failure are sown in success is also true. The following mistakes were self-inflicted and avoidable. They include:

- **Risking authenticity for short-term gains**. In the early 90s, Boston Chicken was a brand that featured gourmet, tasty chicken of superior quality when the company unexpectedly replaced the brand with "Boston Market." Consumers loved the brand of Boston Chicken, willing to pay premium prices and accept minor inconveniences of sometimes long order lines and limited locations. The name change needed to be clarified. Many, like me, wondered about the reason for the change and how we would be affected. Would the business cut the chicken choices on the menu to offer other food? How would service change? Would meals cost more due to the expanded options? Customers did not understand the reason for the name change. Why would any successful business known to everyone change its name? Can you imagine McDonald's keeping the arch but changing its name? Unsurprisingly, the Boston Market brand began to stumble, verging on bankruptcy. Management learned that authenticity is a critical component of personality: If you lose it, the brand is at risk.

- **Modifying positioning strategy.** Changing a brand's positioning is perilous, even to gain more customers. Old Navy was a brand for value-oriented families interested in purchasing its extensive selection of T-shirts, jeans, khakis, and other casual attire. A new chief marketing officer introduced a new line of trendy, inexpensive clothing to appeal to young, fashion-conscious women. Old Navy sales declined more than 20 percent within a few months. Old customers were frustrated and left, and the new positioning did not attract enough new customers to offset the defecting customers. Rolex, the Swiss luxury watchmaker, invested years of marketing in establishing a personality of luxury and sophistication, producing iconic watches designed and manufactured for the most successful businesspeople and athletes. Imagine the impact on sales if the company introduces a Rolex model price for the everyday watch wearer. Fortunately, Rolex management has resisted the urge to tarnish the brand's value.

- **Positioning Inconsistency**. Rebranding and repositioning are complicated, with many examples of failure. One of America's oldest retailers dominated mail-order sales of housing kits, clothing, and home goods known for their quality and durability to pioneers in the mid-to-late 1880s. The company expanded to brick-and-mortar stores specializing in hardware with their Craftsman line in the early-to-mid 1900s. In the early 1990s, Sears discontinued its mail-order service. Craftsman tools underwent design changes, and customers determined they were not as durable as before, losing the brand promise of quality and durability. Sears never recovered.

- **Poor Imitation**. In the early 1980s, Kmart targeted low-price and value customers with their "blue-light specials," putting random products on sale with deep discounts for short times during the day. Walmart offered low prices daily for similar products with a price match guarantee. When Walmart began attracting its customers, Kmart replicated the larger company's discount strategy despite its smaller financial base. Kmart's brand was a shadow of Walmart with no distinct personality. Customers quickly realize the indifferent brands and turn to the brands with defined personalities and positions.

The Hero Brand Difference

Charisma – the ability to attract and influence others – is the intangible combination of style and substance that appeals to our conscious and unconscious minds. Charisma is more than grabbing attention or mesmerizing someone for a moment. It engages consumers psychologically by triggering positive emotions and experiences.

Hero brands have charisma, that special "something" that stands out from the crowd and draws an audience. Charisma is not a gift (although some people may have natural advantages) but the consequence of carefully developed qualities and behaviors. Hero Brands deliberately define and embrace their personality to create an enduring link with their customers.

Consider your favorite Hero Brand and compare its products with those of a competitor:

- Are you willing to pay more, travel a longer distance, or wait longer to get the product or service of your Hero Brand?

- Do you confuse the Hero Brand's products with those of a competitor?

- Do you trust the Hero Brand will meet your expectations anywhere in the world?

- Do you have good memories of the Hero Brand?

- Would you trade it for another brand?

- Do you feel a connection with the brand?

The answers to the questions clarify the meaning of brand personality. A brand is like a person evoking mental pictures of it after multiple encounters. There is no personality without images and associated feelings.

A Hero Brand understands that personality is the connection that keeps the relationship going. Consequently, they embed the companies' implicit promise to continually meet customer expectations in every product, communication, and treatment in their personality.

Delivering on their promises leads to long-term consumer relationships, i.e., brand loyalty.

Brand loyalty benefits the customer and the brand. Higher sales provide the capital for continued enhancements to their products and the security the company needs to make long-term investments in the business.

Hero brands are experts in coordinating their personality and positioning to remain relevant and connected to their consumers long-term by continually reaffirming their personality and positioning strategy. For example, the Four Seasons or Peninsula Hotel brands promote luxury, adventure, and sophistication. Holiday Inns targets family values, fun, and sincerity. Motel 6 has a personality of economy, welcome, and safety.

Hero Brands are global-friendly. While they keep the same fundamental image for brand integrity, they retain the flexibility to adapt to local tastes, cultural preferences, and global trends. They adjust and innovate to local conditions and customer needs without sacrificing their personality, gaining customer loyalty through consistent product delivery and relevance to their customer base. They never change who they are for short-term gain. They design their marketing strategy for growth rather than for revenue.

Summary

The game of *customer experience* and *engagement* has changed. Consumers are more demanding and expect a complete experience. It's not about how good a brand's core business is; it is about complementary features that make the customer experience unique, fulfilled, and satisfying.

The personality of the brand must create an emotional connection with its customers and consistently deliver the brand's promises. Anything less is a failure of personality or positioning. Just like people, changing what you were does not change who you are. You may wear different attire for different occasions, but you will remain who you are. Brands are no different. Sadly, many brands go for the revolution not the evolution which, normally, ends up to be fatal for the brand existence.

Trait 3: Global and Cultural Friendly

"Glocalization" in the effecter merger of international markets and culture relevance. For most of history, distance, mountains, and oceans of sand and water separated communities of people. Each group developed unique and distinct languages, economies, and cultures. National pride and the ideology of "Us and Them" emerged from the combination of physical and sociological barriers and remains as dominant today as then. Technology flattened the mountains and spanned great distances, shrinking the spaces that protected and isolated each society. The world grows smaller.

Globalization – the flow of money, goods, information, and people across national borders and cultures – occurs at a breath-taking pace powered by giant businesses seeking resources and markets. Coca Cola is enjoyed by consumers living in Beijing, Madrid, and Lagos as well as Lima, Liverpool, and Atlanta. McDonald's Golden Arches draws hungry customers from Bakersville, North Carolina to Berlin, Germany. The world devours tacos from Mexico, sushi from Japan, and falafels from Egypt. But globalization is not what it appears for Hero Brands.

In 1983, Harvard Business School professor Theodore Levitt declared that a "global market for uniform products and services had emerged."[i] He argued that corporations should exploit the "economics of simplicity" and sell standardized products all over the world. Levitt argues that business using the strategy would "benefit from enormous economies of scale in production, distribution, marketing, and management."

Twenty years later, while attending graduate school in New York City, my strategy professor, Dr. Prakash Sethi, asserted there are few global brands that sell identical products or services everywhere. Companies going global with a standardization strategy found that foreign consumers had difficulty relating to generic products and marketing programs that discounted their individualities. A subsequent 2004 study in Harvard Business Review[ii] confirmed the problems of one-size-fits-all in international markets.

Today, many companies seek to be a global brand, the ultimate measure of a successful business. They have learned to embrace local and regional differences in their products while including them under their brand's umbrella.

The Value of Glocalization

The optimum positioning of a global brand combines the strength of a household name with products and services modified to meet local cultures and needs. This strategy encompasses their global identity and the nuances of local markets. Recognizing the need for localization can take years.

Several years ago, Apple recognized its global strategy had reached its limits. Despite its technical expertise, the company's global market share for smartphones has consistently ranged in the 14%-16% range, well below Samsung's share of 20%-23%. Overall, Android phones account for 70% of global mobile operating system market. In efforts to reduce costs and lower consumer prices, the company opened manufacturing plants in second tier and emerging economies. They adjusted its global marketing strategy, tweaking language and pictures to target specific markets that did not respond to its generic worldwide campaign.

Hero brands are globally friendly. These are the household names that you love and recognize no matter where you travel. It's as though no boundaries exist, and the entire world is the market. While global-friendly brands are not synonymous with identical replicas, the assurance remains that some similarities exist. The Hero brands recognize that as natural borders become more permeable, people still cling to their small tribal ancestries, and yearn for the comfort of their *local* surrounds – a language they speak and understand, people that look and sound like they do, familiar foods.[iii]

McDonald's Flexibility

For example, when you see a McDonald's, whether it's in Germany, Egypt, UAE, or United States, you know it has an unchanged identity and you can expect a certain level of consistency. This is true considering that the menus between all these locations vary based on local tastes, preferences, and culture.

For example, the Gracoro Burger in Japan contains a patty of macaroni, prawn, and white sauce with a breadcrust crust. In Malaysia, the popular Bubur Ayam McD is a porridge-like dish of chicken strips, spring onions, sliced ginger, fried shallots, and diced chilis. A Big (Maharaja) Mac in India is made with two vegetarian patties while Chinese customers devour Taro Pies, resembling the classic apple fried pie but made with bright purple taro. McDonald's is truly a Hero brand with its ability to adapt to local tastes and customers. Hero brands are not afraid to change to meet the local culture and customer expectations.

Automobiles

While the makes and models might look the same, automobile manufacturers tailor specifications for different parts of the world. A friend of mine starting a new job in Kuwait decided to export his new car from the United States. Within a few days of use, in temperatures of almost 60°C, the car overheated. The car was not designed to operate in hot climates. Had my friend recognized its limits, he could have purchased a model built with GCC specifications, autos specifically designed and manufactured to withstand the extreme weather conditions and rough terrain of the Middle East.

Globalization's first step is (1) understanding the internal and external challenges of the targeted market and (2) recognizing how quickly the brand can adjust to meet the challenges.

Adaptability is Mandatory in Foreign Markets

Hero brands must be chameleons. In addition to being in tune with their customers, they must be flexible enough to satisfy foreign consumers' tastes, habits, values, religious beliefs, language, and local regulations without compromising the brand reputation. Customer tastes vary from region to region and between countries. Only brands that accommodate local preferences and idiosyncrasies succeed in capturing significant market shares.

A Hero brand reflects and personalizes a company's vision. For example, Microsoft's corporate vision is *"to help people and businesses throughout the world realize their full potential.*" This vision statement presupposes that that people and businesses worldwide will use the company's products for their personal or organizational development.[iv] The company also recognized that potential buyers expect personalized journeys in their native language to validate the brand's value. Consequently, Microsoft developed and delivered 9 separate global campaigns in 22 languages to 86 countries during 2022.

Customers react differently to global brands than they do to local brands. This reaction varies depending on the local customs and societal norms. In some cases, customers attribute higher trust and quality from global brands compared to local brands. Conversely, some populations have an inherent distrust of global brands, preferring local ones due to mishaps that can easily occur in foreign markets. Examples of brands committing unforced errors include:

- **General Mills** using Betty Crocker to market cake mixes in Japan. The company's research (or lack thereof) failed to note that Japanese homes do not have ovens. A subsequent effort to substitute rice cookers for the missing ovens also failed.

- **Avon** attempted to enter the Japanese cosmetic markets with their American practice of door-to-door sales. They overlooked the Japanese culture that prioritized privacy in the home and the unwillingness of Japanese housewives to sell products to friends.

- **Home Depot** attempted to expand into China in 2006, failing to note that there is no DIY culture in the country.

No brand intentionally makes a mistake on a global scale, but it can happen to any business that disregards the local culture. Nestlé's drive for international sales les to campaigns suggesting that baby formula was better for babies than breast milk through nursing. Millions of mothers in Third World countries switched to formulas, lacking confidence in their own milk. Millions of babies died of malnutrition that some blamed on the aggressive marketing of the product in under-developed poor countries. Nestlé with its 50% market share suffered a nationwide boycott of its products and subsequently agreed to new marketing messages limited to developed countries.[v]

At the same time, global brands are expected to export the higher standards of their home country to foreign markets. Nike suffered a major backlash from customers when the "sweat shop conditions" of its foreign workforce became public. A film, *Behind the Swoosh*, documented foreign workers in Indonesia, India, Thailand, Bangladesh, and Cambodia being paid $1.25 per day and living in slums near open sewers with shared toilets and bathwater with multiple families. A *Life magazine* article included a picture of a 12-year-old boy sewing a Nike soccer ball. Despite the company's efforts to improve foreign labor conditions, critics claim the improvements are "more of opportunism than benevolence." A brand that fails to adapt their practices to meet world standards of human rights and fairness while accommodating local cultures is easily viewed as insulting, exploitive colonialism.

Consumer Habits and Culture

Global-friendly brands prioritize local consumer habits. Their goal is to become a part of a customer's routine for life by providing an experience more than a simple product or service. Understanding their role in the community enables them to deliver products that contribute to healthy, environmentally friendly ways. Hero brands deliver products and service consistent with the local culture, values, beliefs, and religion.

A Hero restaurant brand does not serve meat in areas where religious beliefs in vegetarianism are held by large segments of the population. Restaurants in Jewish or Islamic communities are kosher and halal, respectively. Europeans prefer bitter drinks that do not appeal to many living in the United States. A Hero brand thoroughly researches foreign markets to understand preferences and taboos prior to entry. They emphasize their commitment and shape the brand by hiring local employees who have an intimate understanding of the culture.

A global-friendly brand fosters friendships in every country they serve. Coca Cola, Microsoft, and other Hero brands have the same image that speaks a hundred languages. A staple on the Cheesecake Factory's menu in Dubai tastes the same at the Cheesecake Factory in the United States. However, the meal in Dubai meets local religious Halal requirements, even though the fundamental recipe required multiple ingredient substitutions and taste tests to deliver the same wonderful flavor. When Olive Garden opened its first unit in UAE, the company removed red wine from its recipes and worked six months to recreate the same taste and textures of the unchanged entrees.

Dunkin Donuts adjusted its menu items to accommodate local preferences as well. They offer pork and seaweed donuts in China and Grapefruit Coolatas in Korea. Even packaging can be as important as price or performance. In Japan, consumers expect Hero brands to be sleek and informative, consistent with their elite status. Such sensitivity and insights reflect local consumers and responses by locally hired managers.

The practice of transferring local managers to oversee the operations in foreign countries was common during my tenure with the Americana Group. Managers neither spoke the language nor related to the local culture. Consequently, the units struggled financially for years without meeting their targeted profits.

Hiring natives who live in the culture has many benefits. No place on earth is immune from constant change and each culture reacts in different ways and pace. Employees from the culture are best suited to understand their customers' reactions and adjust products to better align with those changes. Hero Brands constantly monitor and interpret the ideas, values, and feelings of their targeted customers and react quickly to strengthen and maintain their hard-won exclusivity in their customers' minds.

Religious and Cultural Influence

Religious beliefs are major influences in many cultures. For example, 90% of India's actively observe religion though practicing different religious beliefs (Islam, Hinduism, Buddhism, Jainism, and Sikhism). Each religion has distinct, sometimes conflicting, theologies, so the likelihood of a single brand serving the diverse religious communities is low. In 2017, 37 incidents of hate violence related to cows and religion occurred.[vi] Hindus account for almost 80% of India's population and believe that cows are sacred. They do not eat beef, accounting for McDonald's vegetarian burger.

Islam accounts for almost 15% of Indians (213 million) and is the predominant religion in many parts of the world (1.8 billion). It is a conservative religion with prohibitions for the use of alcohol, the payment of interest, diet, and food preparation. Nike was forced to recall shoes and publicly apologize to the Muslim community in 1997 when the logo on their shoes resembled the word for "God"

Religious sensibilities can make or break a brand's success. Imagine trying to sell risqué clothing when conservative wear is mandated by religious beliefs. One would have more luck selling ice to the arctic research station than selling bacon to a Muslim customer.

Regulatory Environment

Though a brand manages to excel in the local culture by considering customer tastes and consumer habits, varying regulations and laws of countries can be tricky. In the United States, federal, state, and local regulations guide business practices that can impact brand image. Health, sanitation, safety, and fire regulations are vastly different in Kuwait and Bangladesh, many affecting strategies to create a strong brand. Alcoholic consumption is celebrated in family cultures of Germany, France, Italy but restricted in Saudi Arabia and Islamic country. A Hero brands must be flexible enough to accommodate the local laws and customs.

Language

Language use is core converting consumers to life-long loyal customers in Hero brands, the foundation for their reputations. Its misuse often ends in a comedy of errors, subjecting the brand to global ridicule on late night television. Companies often attempt to use the same language across borders, failing to recognize a word can have vastly different meanings in different cultures. For example, Coca Cola in Chinese characters means "Bite the Wax Tadpole."

A word that is praiseworthy in one country can be insulting in another. Figures of speech such as "All hat, no cattle" cause confusion in countries without a cowboy culture, especially when the language is not the first or primary language spoken in the home.

Conversational styles also affect brand communication. A direct approach is preferred in the United States, rude in Asian families, and a bit boring in Spain where digressions enliven communication. Global-friendly brand acceptance is culturally driven. Hero Brands are flexible and adapt to language barriers, customs, tastes, and regulations while maintaining the personality and positioning of the brand.

Summary

Going global successfully requires a tremendous amount of research and preparation with a robust support system. Understanding the intended market and its culture is the first step toward global success. A successful brand speaks the language of the people, feels the pulse of the culture, and stimulates the community's appreciation.

Trait 4: Excel in Operations

As a rule, **Hero brands never disappoint their customers**. They manage expectations and consistently, repeatedly deliver on their promises. How many times have you heard about a recall of a Mercedes or BMW vehicle, a McDonald's being closed due to failed health inspections, or complaints about the appearance or accuracy of a Rolex watch? I suspect that, if you recall the number of incidents involving those brands, you can count them on the fingers of a single hand.

Operations include the policies, processes, and practices that an organization uses to establish a memorable, superior customer experience. Hero brands focus on each element necessary to deliver a positive reaction in every exposure with their consumers. Excellence is not an accident, but the consequence of **a deliberate, carefully managed program** to be the best in their marketplace.

The concept of modern operations management evolved from Sumerian systems to identify, record, and analyze business transactions. Clay tokens and tablets with cuneiform writing from 5000 years in the past are believed to be the first records of business management and written contracts between sellers and consumers.

Since that time, the definition of "operations" expanded to include all aspects of a business from the design, manufacture, and sale of a product or service to the recruitment, selection, and management of workers. The source, price, and transportation of raw materials is included as well as the delivery, transportation, and marketing of products. Managers consider every component of the system – no detail is too small to recognize – to create a satisfying, memorable customer reaction.

The Importance of Operations Management

Operations management is the foundation of a brand. The quality of operations management expands or limits the consumer's view of a brand's product or service. Hero brands understand that a failure of any process in the system damages their credibility and tarnishes the brand. One misstep can undermine years of effort to attain Hero Brand status. **Excellent operations management distinguishes Hero brands from the anonymity and struggles of ordinary brands.** Hero Brands built their market equity on the consumers' trust that their products will consistently and fully meet or exceed expectations.

Readers can find hundreds of books detailed on each aspect of Operations Management, but my objective is limited to identifying specific aspects that directly affect a consumer's confidence in a company's brand. For example, failing to train an employee to deal appropriately with consumer problems is more immediate and consequential than a decision between wo similar raw materials suppliers.

My Burberry Experience

A few years ago, I had a wonderful customer service experience. While on vacation in the United States, my wife and I visited the Burberry shop in New York City. We continued to Maryland where my wife noticed her new handbag was stained and did not respond to the usual cleaning. We stopped in the Burberry store there in the hopes of getting suggestions about removing the stains.

The store manager was more than happy to explain the proper care instructions. Afterward, he took the bag and disappeared. We hoped he would employ some special magical cleaning. To our astonishment, he returned with a new replacement. To say we were impressed and "wowed" would be an understatement.

Neither of us expected the superb customer service, especially since we purchased the bag in a different state. Based on that single incident, Burberry gained two customers for life. Our experience demonstrates how Hero brands exceed customer expectations. Customer service – an element of operational excellence - brings customers back, not the high-resolution advertisement of products.

What is Operational Excellence?

When teaching Operations Management at Baruch College in New York in the early 2000s, I stressed that operations management is not limited to manufacturing, but the behavior of everybody within an organization, from C-level executives to the new hire in the mail department. Operational excellence enhances the company's brand and generates revenue growth. Excellence requires an organization-wide commitment to:

- extraordinary customer experiences,
- an engaged, empowered workforce, and
- standardized (repeatable) processes to ensure minimal failures in scope or impact.

Hero brands sometimes fall short of their promises. For example, the Covid pandemic in 2020 devastated supply lines, adding costs and delays in the availability of thousands of products. While customers recognized the difficulties associated with the virus, many brands strengthened their connection with their customers with unique advertising and actions:

- **Panera Bread**. The restaurant chain advertised new cleaning protocols "including cleaning more frequently and adding additional cleanings with peroxide solution in high-touchpoint locations." The company subsequently offered "contactless delivery," in which it offered placing "mindfully packaged" meals on customers' doorsteps, eliminating any need for contact.

- **McDonald's Philippines**. The Philippines unit created a video where CEO Kenneth Yan detailed the measures the company was taking for the safety of its employees and customers.

- **CVS.** The pharmacy chain introduced innovated video visits with a health professional that permitted patients to "get consultation and support from the comfort of home."

- **Cottonelle.** One of the world's largest toilet paper producers created the #ShareASquare campaign to discourage panic buying by emphasizing togetherness and empathy with the tag line "Stock up on Gratitude."

- **Nike**. The sports shoe manufacturer encouraged customers to "play inside" and stay at home.

- **BMW**. The automobile company sent its "family members," i.e., customers, an email that stressed the importance of "community, togetherness and common purpose."

The examples illustrate that the companies cared for their customers and understood the larger global battle, while still staying consistent with their brand voices. Consumers do not expect perfection, but they remember how a brand responds during difficult events.

Operational excellence requires standardized, distinct processes that are functional and add value to the customer. Unless you have a strong system and culture in place, controlling human error is difficult. Employees ultimately leave organizations to retire or find new opportunities. New people must be taught and continually reminded to continue the established system for a brand to keep its identity and reputation.

Working in the YUM! System taught me the importance of having a solid operational management system and routines in place. Routines are imperative for a brand's relevance. Without consistent patterns of behavior, brands falter and lose equity, identity, and personality, the foundation for a customer's affinity for the brand.

A common mistake of diversified or international organizations is attempting to use the same operations manual for multiple brands, the only difference being the brand name. This approach guarantees that no persistent identity or personality is created. The inevitable happens, and the brand suffers the same fate as Kmart or Sears. Create a system that reflects the brand's intended personality and trust it to succeed.

Great service is always recognized. Failures are typically the result of frontline employees lacking the training and empowerment to resolve issues. Excellent customer service is more than manuals, procedures, flowcharts, and training. It lives in the hearts and minds of employees.

Operations excellence allows brand employees to focus on growth, innovation, customer loyalty, and competitive advantage. As a consultant, my first task when working for a new brand is to determine the functionality, standardization, and consistency of the company's operational management.

What Processes are Included in Operations Management?

Operations Management spans every facet of a company, including recruitment, hiring, training, supply chain management, inventory control, marketing, merchandising strategies, and more. **Strong operating systems must be in place to deliver extraordinary customer experience**s.

While working for the YUM organization during the mid-90s, I attended the company's managerial training program based on the concept of *"Success routines."* The program's objective is to teach managers how to create and practice successful routines for themselves, their subordinates, and the entire organization. What I learned became the foundation of my *back-to-basics program* I now use with my business clients.

My definition of organization excellence is an operating system of routine practices that creates a positive, long-term connection with a consumer. The system continually evolves, i.e., constantly improves, to become perfectly aligned with customer needs and expectations. As such, the system protects the brand's identity and reputation.

Operational excellence does not rely on arbitrary employee behaviors, ethics, or moods. Standardized procedures in a customer-focused culture guides customer interactions and empower employees to be brand ambassadors. **Operational excellence is the confluence of the best people and the best system in place.**

Employee Recruitment and Employment

A company's employees are the delivery system of customer experience. An untrained, unmotivated, or unethical employee can destroy a perfect system. Conversely, their counterparts can make companies best-in-class – the Hero brands. Having systems in place to identify, recruit, evaluate, and hire the best candidates is essential for thoroughness, cost, and efficiency of the HR process. But a system is not enough; it must be documented in some manner - a handbook, manual, flow-chart, standard operating procedures (SOP), policies – to be repeatable and improved.

Companies often select candidates for experience, not character. The former can be learned on the job, the latter is integral to one's personality. Trust between the brand and its customers is essential to the long-term survival and success of an organization. The objective of recruitment and employment is securing the right candidates who will enhance and support the brand image.

Hero brands know that **employees are the key to the success of an organization.** They focus on each employment candidate's leadership traits and attitude. Seek the same attributes when working in international markets but limit your candidates to locals who speak the language and understand the culture, the consumers' behavior, and their preferences.

Tesco, a very successful British grocery store chain, abandoned the U.S market in 2012 after suffering losses of $1.6 billion. While the language difference between British and American English were not significant, the company **failed to understand the U.S. grocery store customs**. The British company failed to consider Americans' preference of in-store coupons or to implement a customer loyalty program. Their stores were one-fifth the size of American grocery stores with store-branded goods packed in small quantities, all practices popular in Britain, but contrary to American habits. Combined with poor locations and the use of self-service check-out machines (Americans prefer dealing face-to-face with cashiers), the expansion had little chance of success.[vii]

Employee Training

My first employer understood the importance of new employee orientation. I and other recruits endured more than four hours of group mind-numbing, bland videos during my first day at work. I do not remember anything after the first 20 minutes other than extreme boredom. The company never bothered to ask the new employees about the effectiveness of the program or how it might be improved, apparently satisfied that the presence of any training was sufficient. Offering the program was simply a box the HR department could check to prove their commitment to employee communications.

Hero brands emphasize training and constantly seek to maximize its value to trainees and the organization. They realize that training is the basis of learning and employee engagement. Training processes, whether for skill improvement or acculturation, require standardization and continual updating of curriculum and delivery to ensure the proper messages are transmitted and received by the workforce.

Effective long-term learning is the first step toward empowering the front line. Hero brands provide training resources – usually from the HR Department with input from operating departments – and expect employees to achieve proficiency without direct supervision.

Online courses are increasingly popular, sometimes supplemented with group classes and individual mentoring. The combination allows employees to proceed at their own pace with automated testing and record-keeping to verify competence and understanding of subject matters. Technology continues to advance, making training more efficient, effective, and available (Smartphone applications).

Business Forecasting

The importance of projecting future business conditions cannot be overstated. Anticipating future economic conditions, sales volumes, costs, capital expenditures, and cash flows is critical for operating strategies today that influence operating decisions tomorrow. In its simplest terms, forecasting is the process of anticipating a brand's future needs. Forecasting allows organizations to be proactive, rather than reactive.

Hero brands constantly collect and analyze data to predict events and conditions that might affect the brand. Accurate forecasts are necessary to

1. Estimate future financial requirements,
2. Establish goals and plans,
3. Improve resource allocations,
4. Anticipate market changes,

5. Create opportunities for growth, and
6. Identify economic and competitive threats to the business.

Supply Chain

Hero Brands understand their customer base and encapsulate those values in their supply chain. Many brands have reconfigured their supply chains due to consumer complaints about their suppliers and production practices:

- **McDonald's**. The fast-food giant discontinued the purchase of chickens raised using antibiotics intended for humans. Tyson, one of the firm's major suppliers, subsequently halted their practice to remain in McDonald's good graces.

- **Ikea**. The world's largest consumer of wood announced plans to buy only wood produced by "responsibly managed forests" and rely solely on recycled wood by 2030.

- **Nike**. The athletic shoe manufacturer faced multiple consumer complaints about its support of foreign sweatshops and agreed to play a role in bringing about positive, systemic change for workers within our supply chain and in the industry."

- **Best Buy**. After complaints from Greenpeace Canada, the company agreed to replace its paper supplier - Resolute Forest Products of Canada – due to its logging practices and destruction of forests.

- **Lego**. The toy maker agreed to cease sales through Shell gas stations following a major oil spill in the Arctic.

- **General Mills**. After complaints about genetically modified (GMO) grains, the cereal maker reformulated many of its existing products and added a line of non-GMO cereals.

Operational excellence requires finding the best supplier that brings the most value to the brand and its intended customers. In many cases, the costs are higher but provide greater value due to their perceived social responsibility.

Being local and global friendly is a trait of Hero Brands, particularly for the food and beverage industry. Franchisors that insist on securing raw materials from their home countries to maintain product authenticity are not Hero brands. A Hero brand develops local suppliers of the same quality as their home country's raw materials. Brands that import basic ingredients typically prioritize product rebate revenue above product standards.

Some industries like automobile manufacture are exceptions. An automobile consists of more than 4,000 separate parts and accounts for as much as fifty percent of its total cost. Many countries, including the United States, assess high tariffs for foreign-produced parts, while others establish various percentage of import costs to total domestic price to avoid a tariff. American auto parts makers don't have capacity to build all the parts domestically that are currently imported. Most imported auto parts are made in Mexico and other low-wage countries.

Another example of an exception is the clothing and textile industry. Raw materials can encompass up to 70% of the total garment cost. High-end luxury brands tend to import from their home base as part of their exclusivity.

Hero clothing brands outsource their suppliers from a few recognizable countries, regardless of the country where the product is sold. In most cases, Hero brands help their distributors maximize profit, potentially harming sales volume, by constantly lowering the cost of the raw product.

Inventory

Inventory at some level is unavoidable. Prior to Covid, many companies employed a **Just-in-Time** inventory strategy. By requiring suppliers to deliver smaller volumes frequently, manufacturers forced their suppliers to assume the costs and responsibilities of storage and logistics. Companies with Hero brands employed the strategy through extensive automated networks with suppliers.

Companies like the retailer Walmart link their store point-of-sale machines with suppliers. When items reach a pre-determined level, the supplier automatically delivers additional stock and avoids empty shelves. Just-in-time delivery was considered a retailer's perfect solution to inventory management, reducing the need for product forecasts, and lowering costs (for the buyer).

The Just-in-Time strategy generally extended and complicated supply lines, often weakening suppliers unable to pass their new costs of storage and logistics. The price of many products became increasingly volatile during periods of economic unrest. The Covid pandemic shattered supply lines with many raw materials unable for months.

For example, the supply of semiconductor chips typically provided by Far East manufacturers was interrupted for months.   The shortage cost global auto manufacturers an estimated $210 billion in 2021 while driving the price of used cars to historic highs. Few industries escaped the impact of supply chain failures. Consequently, "Just-in-Time" inventory practices became "Just-in-Case," effectively a return to the practice of holding large amounts of inventory on hand and nearby their consumption. The importance of accurate forecasts returned.

Inventory strategies and accounting methods are industry- or company- specific. The Financial Accounting Standards Board (FASB) allows several inventory calculation methods including the "last in, first out," "retail inventory," "first in, first out," and "average cost." Companies choose the method that best gives them tax or strategic advantage.

Hero brands were quick to recognize the problem with extended, elaborate supply chains and moved to reduce their impact on operations and customers. International Hero brands emphasized local suppliers, sometimes reconfiguring their products or services to meet the new conditions. Brands unwilling or unable to adopt new practices continue to suffer. In an increasingly volatile market, they are exposed to future calamities.

Site Selection

Site selection is a critical issue for most businesses. Decision makers must balance market (customer access), workforce (potential employees), financial factors (facility costs, taxes, logistical access), and surrounding infrastructure. The final choice employs sophisticated research and metrics to optimize benefits and limit disadvantages of a site. Following the opening of a site, research continues to verify the analysis and modify factors as needed to reflect actual results.

Choosing the right location for an international business can make the difference between success and failure. Hero brands constantly adjust and improve their criteria to identify the best sites most suited to their projected customers' expectations of the brand. For example, a Rolex store located next to Saks Fifth Avenue fits the brand personality. A Rolex kiosk situated in the middle of a neighborhood shopping center would diminish the image of the brand.

Home Depot's expansion into China failed because they did not understand the culture including the location of their targeted customers. Home Depot build stores away from the major population centers in China, replicating their site strategy in the United States. Home Depot stores in the U.S. are typically located in the suburbs where affluent people are more likely to live. They failed to consider that the Chinese affluent generally prefer rented apartments and condominiums in the cities, including staffs responsible for repairs and maintenance.

Employee Staffing and Engagement

Labor management can be difficult but rewarding. When things go well, they frequently exceed expectations. A failure can quickly become disastrous, negatively affecting hard won consumer trust. Hero brands focus labor management on positive customer experience. Operational excellence requires more than adequate staffing; employees must be empowered to resolve customer issues efficiently and effectively.

Determining the appropriate staffing levels is a process to balance costs and customer experience. Excessive staff might improve customer satisfaction but adds excessive costs and reduces profits. Conversely, minimal staffing reduces costs but endangers customer satisfaction. Reaching the optimum balance between the two is especially difficult since employees are rarely 100% productive and a small percentage of customers are impossible to satisfy.

Employees have most of the responsibilities to deliver the brand promises and build the brand equity and market credibility. Too much emphasis on labor saving can backfire as I found when working as an area manager in 2000 for Pizza Hut in New York.

Faith, one of our restaurant managers, had difficulty meeting her sales targets. With declining sales, unit profits began to fall. She reacted by cutting staff, intending to personally assume their duties. On the day of my visit, I found her struggling to answer five phones. Finding themselves on hold, many customers simply hung up, a lost sale in each case. I realized the cause of declining sales. Faith was figuratively burning the furniture to warm the house, hoping that the winter would quickly end.

At my direction, she immediately reinstated the terminated employees plus one. The strategy of one extra employee became a rule "Needed Staff +1." In the fast-food industry, customer service is everything. Requiring customers to endure long wait times on the phone or waiting for their order inevitably leads to lower sales.

A month later, Faith's unit experienced double-digit sales growth and met her financial targets. The improvement continued, so that Faith received company recognition awards instead of her former performance action plans.

During my remaining time with Pizza Hut, I reminded Faith that a ringing phone or a customer at the door is money knocking at the door. Companies choose to collect or ignore it. With adequate staff plus one, there is always an employee to greet a guest, answer a ringing phone, or complete transactions faster. An extra employee provides an opportunity to go the extra mile to satisfy your customers.

In some cases, extra workers may not be available due to schedules, lack of training, or excessive costs. Consequently, Hero brands extend labor productivity by continuous employee training and technological innovation. Typical examples include the expanded use of automated, customer-directed ordering and payment in restaurants and supermarkets. While automation reduces costs and expands customer involvement, the impersonal service and reduced human presence can weaken the link between brand and customer.

Walmart is an industry leader deploying technology to manage their business and maintain customer service. The technology works because Walmart trains its employees to use it effectively. Without the training and the full support of management, technology would be useless.

Operational excellence necessitates continuous efforts to promote the connections between employees, products, and customers, despite decreases in personal interactions. A Hero brand located in Louisville; Kentucky in the United States has successfully created an unbreakable bond between the three components.

Americans love baseball. Consumers worldwide recognize the image of a baseball bat, an indispensable tool of the game. Hillerich & Bradley Company has been manufacturing bats in a single location since the mid-1890s under the brand "Louisville Sluggers." The iconic brand is recognized anyplace the game is played, even though company employees rarely interact with customers.

The success of the "Louisville Sluggers' is based on the consistent high quality and affordability of the products year after year. During a 2005 visit to the manufacturing facility, I learned that employee turnover was extremely low, the shortest tenure of the workforce being eleven years. A significant number of the employees have worked at the facility thirty-five years!

The employees at Louisville Slugger are fully engaged in the company's Mission:

"The bat business is complex, and Louisville Slugger's product assortment and marketing strategy, specifically, are designed to help players weather the complexity to find the product that's right for them. "

The employees at Hillerich & Bradley Company take pride in their product and the brand's history. The company is an excellent example of how a Hero brand excels in operations by retaining its loyal and most experienced employees.

Summary

Operations excellence is the most complicated and demanding attribute of a brand. The success of a brand rises and falls on how the brand's operations are consistently executed. Human involvement and interactions complicate the operations of a business. A single careless act, misstatement, or misunderstanding magnified by the power of social media can destroy a brand. A strong, well-defined operating system minimizes the risk of improvisation by guiding employees to value and preserve connections with consumers. Hero brands emphasize organizational excellence everywhere the brand operates.

Trait 5: Scalable

Scalability has numerous definitions. For the purposes of this book, scalability refers to the flexibility of a brand to offer multiple options that tap into any market without losing its personality or identity. Scalability is critical for the long-term viability of a brand. It is a differentiator between brands designed for a short-term gain or limited vision and those who understand market dynamics and global market needs.

Starbucks

As of September 2023, Starbucks, the world's largest coffee house chain, has almost 38,000 stores in approximately 80 countries. The company began in a 1,000-square-foot store front space in Seattle with a single employee. The company's scalability is based on consistent product quality and a unique ability to create a special ambiance in its customers' minds, regardless of physical location.

The brand prides itself on the ability of its store designs to fit into and enhance a community. It offers everything from dedicated small spaces within retail stores to a mid-size outlet in an airport to a larger stand-alone restaurant. The freestanding locations can be situated on as little as 0.50 acres and up to 2,000 square feet to provide a cozy, intimate setting. The brand's largest coffee facility is in Seattle, Washington, on a 15,000-square feet parcel of land.

Subway

Hero Brands offer numerous prototypes to ensure continual growth. Subway, the world's largest single-brand restaurant chain, began in 1965 in a small shop serving custom sandwiches of long, split bread rolls filled with meat, cheese, vegetables, and dressings made onsite to a customer's specifications. Today, the company has over 44,000 locations in 100 countries. Subway⊡ stores differ in size and are found everywhere including worship facilities, high schools, and cruise ships.

The availability of multiple prototypes enables them to forego any locations in extremely pricey real estate areas, even if they exhibit high traffic.

Subway is a classic example of scalability. The smallest Subway location is in Honolulu, Hawaii, and can only serve a couple of customers at a time. The largest Subway is in Jamestown, North Carolina. It encompasses 6,668 square feet and accommodates at least 211 customers. This brand has found a way to fit anywhere, including a worship facility, high school, boats, and even temporary construction sites. As discussed in previous chapters, standardized operations lead to an efficient environment that makes scalability possible.

The Competitive Advantage of Scalability

Scalability is the sum of all the moving parts. Knowledge of their customer base and market enables Hero brands to retain their personality and accomplish extraordinary growth simultaneously. The scalability of Hero Brands allows them to thrive during different economic times in different retail environments with a combination of mass appeal and exclusivity under the same brand identity. All Hero brands share the ability to scale geographically.

Typically associated with technology and Hero brands like Google, Apple, and Microsoft, geographical scalability is present in multiple industries such as hospitality, retail, fashion, food, and beverage. Geographical scalability refers to the flexibility of a brand to establish a successful business regardless of location or size. For example, the management of Chili's restaurants designs facilities to fit the space available, from a limited menu and minimal seating space in a busy airport to a full-service, stand-alone restaurant where square footage is available.

Why is Scalability Key to Hero Brands?

Scalability is a necessary component of the long-term viability of a brand. It is a differentiator between brands designed for a short-term gain or limited vision and others who understand the market dynamics and the global market needs. Managers of Hero brands purposefully plan for scalability in the earliest stages of their growth.

Walmart

Walmart, the retail store chain, is an example of designed scalability. Today, the company's stores include:

- **Sam's Club warehouses**. Sam's Club is a wholesale membership warehouse and encompasses approximately 12% of the brand's locations.

- **Supercenters**. As of 2016, two-thirds of over 11,500 Walmart stores are Supercenters, each encompassing 260,000 square feet.

- **Walmart Discount Centers**. The centers were the original Walmart mode, averaging 106,000 square feet. Less than 8% of the store locations remain Walmart Discount Stores.

- **Neighborhood Markets**. These smaller, corner-store locations, typically in urban neighborhoods, average 38,000 square feet in size and represent 13% of Walmart Brand locations.

- **Small Formats**. The design promotes the sale of Walmart products and services on college campuses and stand-alone gas stations. Less than 0.7% of all locations are the Smaller Format prototype.

A network of 172 distribution centers strategically located on a regional basis serves the retail locations.

Scaling through small outlets can grow a brand's equity faster. In addition to faster brand recognition, opening smaller outlets typically translates into higher ROIs through lower investment and operating costs. In some instances, the ability of the brand to utilize multiple design prototypes is the only possible way to grow globally and become scalable.

How do Hero Brands Showcase Scalability?

While Hero Brands take slightly different approaches to implementing scaling, they all successfully do it. Different prototypes that accommodate any market or location are one such trend. Most franchise operations are inherently scalable due to their established models.

McDonald's

McDonald's management brand did not initially view its brand as scalable due to real estate constraints - a widespread problem in the food and retail industry. McDonald's perfected its business model and operations management before it started thinking about scalability through franchising. During the 1960s to 1970s, the company shifted its focus to operations management to maintain brand integrity and consistency among its locations, whether company-owned or franchised.

Undoubtedly, McDonald's is a Hero brand and meets all the criteria. It has more than 36,000 locations in over one hundred countries worldwide. McDonald's has a consistent look, feel, and primary menu. Nevertheless, the company tailors the menu and facility design to its location.

In the past, McDonald's locations sought locations near a corner on a signalized intersection for heightened access and visibility. Each site must comply with local building and planning regulations, ordinances, and codes and consider matters like customer parking and supplier deliveries.

The brand establishes the minimum height, building size, and parcel size for stand-alone locations and the options for stores located in malls or retail stores. In general, the smaller the facility, the smaller (less choice) the menu. Nevertheless, no matter what McDonald's prototype you see, you always know it is a McDonald's.

Consistency is Critical

That recognition is a characteristic of all Hero brands. They always maintain the brand's identity, personality, or positioning when they switch from one prototype to another.

Hertz

Consistency of the brand across the various prototypes helps to build identity, equity, and customer loyalty. Hertz car rental brand is scalable and consistent throughout its different international locations. Regardless of location, the Hertz product, website, service, and layout are the same. Hertz locations within another business, such as an airport or car dealership, will have a similar theme that keeps the brand recognizable.

Hero Brands do not arise by chance. They are carefully managed to capitalize on their customers' needs and wants. Applying the concept of customer knowledge correctly allows organizations to achieve excellence, development, and competitive advantage.

Brinks

Brinks provides secure transport and associated security services in more than 100 countries.   The company's customer intelligence systems have generated a wealth of product usage information since 1994; its call centers have accumulated voluminous historical customer-level transaction data; and its field reps have been gathering competitive data since it began operations.

Brinks wanted to find a way to use all this information to accelerate growth and optimize every customer touchpoint across all channels, especially in its messaging, personalization, and delivery of the user experience. In the fall of 2020, the company reorganized its structure around customer acquisition, service, and renewal and began using Artificial Intelligence (AI) to optimize service-call scheduling, help cross-sell recommendations from call center reps, and personalize every customer touchpoint.

How do I Know When a Brand is Scalable?

Not all businesses are scalable. Scalable businesses have increasing revenue while operating costs stay the same (or require little additional cost). Eighty percent of new businesses fail during the growth phase because they are not scalable. Not all successful brands meet the criteria for a Hero brand. Heroes can continue to grow and prosper regardless of the location because their multiple prototypes fit any scenario and provide consistency to retain brand identity and personality. It remains visible and accessible to customers since the prototypes cover small-, medium-, and large-scale outlets.

KFC

KFC is another Hero brand in the food and beverage industry that has mastered scalability. While it has humble beginnings in Louisville, Kentucky, the brand now has close to 30,000 locations in 150 countries. Approximately 99% of new facilities were franchises.

KFC established facility standards as an integral part of its branding. There are two preferred outlet sizes, but a new location requires a minimum of 0.45 acres to accommodate the building and parking. The YUM! Brands have combined two brands (such as KFC and Pizza Hut) into a single restaurant with a shared drive-thru. KFC is also found in a mall food court or as part of a gas station.

Generally, brands have fewer large flagship stores than smaller stores. During my career with YUM! Brands, I opened KFC facilities from 400 square feet to 4000 square feet. All were profitable, and each one maintained the integrity of the KFC brand. Real estate is not getting any cheaper, so the decision to open a facility sometimes comes down to its location. Scalability provides an avenue to enter the market regardless of real estate costs.

Hilton

The hospitality industry is another example of scalability employing sub-brands. Hilton Worldwide Holdings, Inc. encompasses fourteen sub-brands and 570 locations in about every country. In order of percentage from highest to lowest, the fourteen brands rank:

1. Hampton (43.57%),
2. Hilton Garden Inn (14.23%),
3. Hilton Hotels and Resorts (11.62%),
4. DoubleTree (9.66%),
5. Homewood Suites (7.57%),
6. Embassy Suites (4.63%),
7. Home2 Suites (1.41%),
8. Hilton Grand Vacation (0.91%),
9. Curio (0.77 %),
10. Conrad Hotels and Resorts (0.5%),
11. Waldorf Astoria Hotels and Resorts (0.5%),
12. Canopy (0.02%),
13. Tapestry Collection (0%), and
14. Tru (0%).

While Hilton is the mother brand, its sub-brands maintain its integrity and reinforce Hilton's positioning as a Hero Brand. Based on the locations, demographics, and targeted customers, Hilton chooses the sub-brand that best satisfies the target market. Many customers only know the mother brand if they read the fine lines stating that Hilton operates the hotel.

The luxury brands are fewer in number but located in prime vacation destinations. These brands include the Waldorf Astoria Hotels and Resorts, Conrad Hotels and Resorts, Canopy, and Tapestry Collection. Each of these brands targets a different customer and caters to an experience.

- Hilton Grand Vacations caters to the high-end market, timeshare market, and families.

- The mid-size market includes Curio, Tru, and DoubleTree.

- The economy market includes Hilton Garden Inn, Embassy Suites, and Hampton.

- The extended stay market has Home2 Suites and Homewood Suites.

The scalability factor of this Hero Brand means it will thrive during the worst of economic times, have both mass appeal and a niche customer, and maintain the same brand identity. Having multiple prototypes is indispensable if a brand wants to go global and thrive in London, Paris, Dubai, and New York.

Summary

Scalability is a vital piece of qualifying for a Hero Brand. A brand or franchise that offers a one-size-fits-all product has limited scalability. An assortment of choices is generally beneficial. However, Hero brands typically operate in multiple geographic markets and offer selections within selections to provide better chances for continual growth.

Scalability promotes market penetration and high visibility for Hero brands, building brand equity faster.

During economic downturns, smaller prototypes with lower operational costs facilitate continued growth with less risk.

Trait 6: Value Driven

All businesses aim for profitability to ensure long-term viability. Otherwise, they will cease to function as a business. Profits are the short-term result of business activities. Profitability is a measure of efficiency; the profits earned relative to the business size. A company must produce profits efficiently to be competitive and deliver sustained value to shareholders and customers.

Revenues and profitability are not the same, but they are related. The combination of the product price and its volume of sales drive revenues. Profitability is the difference between revenues and costs. Company leaders constantly seek to maximize the gap between revenues and costs.

The profit formula never changes. Whether a Fortune 500 company or a local grocery store, profit equals total revenue minus cost.

How can profits be increased?

Companies typically increase profits by:

1. Increasing revenue while maintaining the same expense levels,
2. Lowering expenses to increase profit margins, or
3. Growing sales and operational efficiency.

Hero Brands generally employ #3 to improve long-term, positive cash flow and increase profits.

Revenue growth reflects the health of a business and the basis for increased profitability and market share. Samsung focused on innovation to increase sales while improving operations efficiency to become an industry leader. Nokia, the previous leader, steadily lost market share by emphasizing short-term revenue growth while restricting innovation to cut costs.

How does a brand increase revenue?

Hero Brands have mastered the ability to increase revenue through one or more of the following strategies:

- Increasing the number of sales transactions per unit,

- Increasing the average sales receipt, i.e., spend per transaction,

- Introducing new products with higher profit margins,

- Entering new markets (geographic expansion), and

- Opening more units in geographical markets (unit density).

Subway increased its market penetration and density through franchising. McDonald's expanded globally to new markets. Apple's growth strategy relies on a continuous stream of new products with higher margins. The company is especially adept at creating demand for new product features, sometimes before customers realize their need for their benefits. Steve Jobs, one of Apple's founders, once said, "I don't think Graham Bell researched the market before inventing the telephone." In other words, **if there is no existing demand, create it**. The strategy worked well as Apple overcame Nokia's industry-leading mobile phone market share.

Adding new products or expanding into new markets is diversification. Walmart is constantly adding new products to give buyers more choices while YUM! offers diverse brands to satisfy different tastes.

A brand cannot reach Hero status if it focuses solely on short-term revenues. Marketing for short-term gain confuses brand identity and leads to irrelevancy. Discounting prices may deplete excessive inventory or temporarily increase cash flow. However, lost profits typically accompany the lower prices, and any increase in market share is temporary.

Effective long-term marketing strategies differentiate Hero Brands from other brands. Their market plans target new customers while retaining old ones to capture market share. Market share drives revenues, not vice versa.

The pizza giant Domino's efforts for the last few years prioritized a better consumer experience. In 2014, Domino's rolled out its version of Apple's Siri, a smartphone-dwelling personal assistant ready to tend to the user's every pizza need. The company has tinkered with delivery robots in Australia and drone delivery in New Zealand. The company's flashy DXP "super-delivery" car, updated to an electric version, has a built-in warming oven and space for 80 pizzas.

For years, the brand was the underdog to Pizza Hut. In 2021, Domino's grabbed the largest share of the pizza chain market in the United States. Their achievement illustrates the value of an innovative long-term strategy. Chick-fil-A has similarly overtaken KFC in the fried chicken chain market.

How does a brand improve operations efficiency?

Improving operations efficiency is a relentless pursuit in business. Hero Brands understand this is an important component of the holistic picture. As previously mentioned, this means improving productivity, adjusting supply chains, or expanding customer service. In restaurants, for example, it is desirable to keep the *big two* costs of food and labor below 50%. Hero Brands strive to keep the costs under 45%. In retail, these percentages correlate with a higher EBITDA.

Brands can only grow to a certain point when a market becomes saturated. Once the market turns into maturity, Hero Brands continue to grow by expanding globally or improving the efficiency of their local operations. A great model of global expansion is the KFC brand. As domestic markets mature, growing globally is the only way to sustain profitability and increase market share, especially in China and the Middle East.

David Novak, previous CEO at YUM! once said that if he had the choice, he would keep the China division and sell the rest. The China division accounted for almost all YUM!'s growth in the last 10 years. It shouldn't be a surprise that the division became YUM China in 2015, a separate entity for YUM!

What are some of the ways to improve operations efficiency that keep brands floating in fierce competition markets, improve profitability and increase cash flow? My following tips to improve productivity and efficiency may seem odd or unexpected:

- Hire individuals with the best attitude - ones that keep a smile on their face when things get rough - and pay them well.

- Choose front-line managers that can run your company in ten years.

- Train for primary and secondary responsibilities. Well-trained, passionate employees can save you up to 30% of your labor cost.

- Recognize, recognize, and recognize employee contributions. There is nothing more rewarding than saying thank you. It is that simple!

- Forecast right, schedule right and order right.

- Collect now and pay later—Dell style.

- Reduce inventory to a minimum and negotiate every price. A dollar saving in one SKU is a million-dollar saving for one million SKU—Walmart style.

- Hire the best talent for procurement and logistics. Getting shipments out as quickly as possible can save millions of dollars over time. It is the little things we overlook that raise costs.

- Choose your size. Big stores with employees standing around are like a 1000-seat theater with only the front row occupied. Don't burn cash. Choosing the right size from the beginning will make your operations efficient. It is better to have a full restaurant with some waiting time than having a huge restaurant with only a few tables filled. Rent, labor, electricity, and food burn cash every minute. Don't make everyone else rich except you.

- Improve communication between different departments. Lots of money is wasted every day simply because people within the same company don't speak to one another.

- Select your area managers or operations managers carefully and pay them well. I have always said, "Give me a great area manager; I will give you great operations." Middle managers can make or break a company.

- Reach out to your front-line employees regularly. The best ideas come from those who feel the pain and look for the gain.

Most industries have developed benchmarks that allow an organization to gauge how it is performing compared to its competition. Hero Brands lead the pack and perform better than the benchmarks established. These companies end up with higher profits and greater profitability. One common benchmark among the food and beverage, retail, and hospitality industries is EBITDA, which represents the earnings before interest, taxes, depreciation, and amortization. Its use enables comparisons between companies regardless of accounting methodology.

Hero Brands yield between 15% and 20% EBITDA, and many exceed the upper end of the range. EBITDA fluctuates depending on outside influences such as economic conditions and varies based on the industry norms. Hilton, for example, reported an adjusted EBITDA of 15.4% from 2013 to 2014.

Adidas had an increase of 28% EBITDA between 2015 and 2016. The "Retail and Consumer Insights 2015 Financial Benchmarking" report showed that Hero Brands doubled their earnings before interest and taxes between 2013 and 2014 whereas struggling brands had negative earnings during the same period (PWC 2015). EBITDA growth is a measure of financial health of a brand. Hero Brands consistently grow EBITDA using multiple methods we mentioned earlier.

Creating a Competitive Advantage

In 2006, I assumed the general management of a Hero Brand's Mid-Atlantic region of the United States, an operation without profits in the previous eleven years. Customer counts plummeted due to understaffing and poor service. Even Hero Brands lose value by neglecting operations and employee morale.

Implementing an operating strategy with a proven record for obtaining good results, I turned the region from a value destroyer to a value creator by the end of 2008. My **"Twelve Initiatives for Twelve Months"** are:

1. **Build a team of individuals who are hungry for success.** Choose enthusiastic, ambitious team members that embrace your passion for business and personal growth to create an unbeatable team.

2. **Assign individuals where they fit culturally in line with their personalities and strengths.**

3. **Eliminate fast the "nay-sayers" - those who inevitably drag down performance and morale.** Give each person a chance to get on board. If they resist, leave them behind. Unfortunately, leaders must make the tough call of who will remain on the bus and who must get off. A concept Jim Collins highlighted in his book "Good to Great".

Removing them early rather than delaying the inevitable for years is best.

4. **Align long- and short-term goals, then delegate performance to team members.** Sharing long and short-term strategic goals with your team allows them to focus their passion on the same objectives.

5. **Trust but verify.** Performance measurement is not a sign of mistrust but a measure of progress. Success follows failure, analysis, and correction.

6. **Create a Reward/ Discipline system.** Employees want to stay where they are valued, so praise often and publicly. Incentivize your top performers. Be consistent in praise and disciplinary actions.

7. **Implement an efficient operations system.** With the right people in place and everybody on the same page, focus your efforts on improving the efficiency of the operating system. Ensure there are enough employees to handle the process and deliver the expected customer experience, even if it means hiring staff.

8. **Avoid micromanaging your employees or sales.** Instead, focus on micromanaging expenses and behavior. Micromanagement inevitably leads to higher staff turnover, greater absenteeism, and poor customer experience. Employees lose confidence, and there is no room for innovation.

9. **Get involved in your team's lives.** Touch their hearts and give credit when the credit is due. Actively build rapport with your team members by learning about their lives away from work. Take care of your people first, and sales and profit will follow. (YUM! style)

10. **Design your marketing strategy for growth.** Develop short-term and long-term marketing tactics to maximize growth and guide you and your team toward profitability.

11. **Walk** the **talk.** Trust is not given but earned from customers, employees, and shareholders. Leadership is not always sunshine and rainbows. Stressful periods always test the bonds of trust between leadership and teams. Having a history of honesty and transparency is critical to building trust.

12. **Staff for growth.** During declining sales, many companies lay off staff to limit losses. Consequently, customer service decreases, customer experience deteriorates, and sales fall faster. The key to reducing poor results is generating more growth by improving customer experience.

The advantage of a Hero Brand is its reservoir of customer loyalty. Customers will overlook short-term service failures if they are quickly corrected.

This strategy works during difficult times. In 2009, the Middle East economies suffered a significant downturn (as did the US). Businesses closed, and many lost their jobs. Even Hero Brands struggled. Some types of adversity occur without warning, forcing companies to react short-term. On such occasions, the goal is to stay afloat until the economy recovers.

A year after I moved to Dubai, the local economy stalled. I initially micromanaged operations in the emergency to create as many cost savings as possible and combat the declining sales. We had to get inventive with every department in the organization finding untraditional ways to save money.

Fortunately, the equity in the Hero Brand gave us time to react and get ahead of the problem. Economies typically have a transition period between booms and busts. The pressures of falling revenues and profits force management to put out fires, losing focus on the customer.

They concentrate on internal issues and the status quo, weakening their connection with customers when that relationship is most critical. Non-Hero Brands cut staff and marketing programs to stop the bleeding, essentially burning the furniture to heat up the house. As a Hero Brand, we cut costs by $20 million in 2009 without jeopardizing our customer base.

How Do You Hold on to the Competitive Advantage?

Never let up and continue pushing the envelope further. The minute you get complacent - patting your back about your brand position - is the minute the brand is at its most vulnerable. Whenever you begin to feel safe, remember Blockbuster management's arrogance in dealing with Netflix. Maintaining a competitive advantage requires constant diligence and keeping sight of future objectives.

Hero Brands understand opportunity costs.

While lecturing about profitability at Baruch College in New York, I had fun with students explaining the opportunity cost. Each term, I began my lesson with a story about a man with a job earning $50,000 a year who suddenly inherited a restaurant. He quit his job to manage the operation and made $75,000 in profit in the first year.

"Did the man make the right financial decision?" I asked. Invariably, the students asserted that taking over the restaurant was the better outcome. "Yes, it was right because he made $25,000 more than the earnings from his old job.

My next question deflated their ego. "What if the heir had kept his job and rented the restaurant for $150,000 annually?" I always laughed when the room filled with "Oops" expressions. The additional $25,000 was so attractive that they never considered other possibilities to use the inheritance to earn more.

In business slang, they left $125,000 "on the table," capital that could be reinvested and earn even more. Companies focus exclusively on EBITDA growth without considering lost opportunities that might produce higher returns.

Consumers Perceived Value

Many brands mistakenly believe that value is equivalent to cost, i.e., a lower price means lower quality. This myth endures among brands trying to gain market share and increase sales. They forget that consumers know the difference between what cheap and value signifies.

Consumers seek the best experience for the right price, the critical difference being *the right price.* Delivering the best experience at the right price is the most challenging problem in business, especially when maintaining a healthy profit margin.

Brands often struggle with pricing strategies when competitive pressure rises. Slower-than-expected growth tempts casual dining restaurants to offer fast-food prices. Five-star hotels discount room rates to three-star hotel prices. Lower-end brands supplement products and services with amenities and gimmicky promotions. Hero Brands recognize the temptation but never compromise brand positioning or profitability.

Summary

Hero Brands practice efficiency and productivity in every aspect of the business, avoiding leaving money on the table. Use the multiple methods discussed in this chapter to increase revenue and improve operational efficiency. Prioritize the customers in your plans. Include them as part of the family of the brand. Work toward globalization. Invest in your employees and treat them as an invaluable part of the brand. They are the ones who deliver the brand promises to your customers. Take a broad approach toward sales and micromanage the expenses. Avoid letting inventory take over. Most importantly, strive for greater value for the organization to create a better-perceived value for your customers, employees, and shareholders.

Trait 7: Mass Appeal

Creating an emotional connection with customers is critical in building a loyal customer base. Brands attract customers with emotional and functional associations. Hero brands are especially adept at creating positive associations in consumers' minds. The most successful become generic equivalents for the functions they provide, including:

- Uber and "short-term, contract transportation."

- Google and "internet search."

- Xerox and "paper copying."

When you need to send an overnight package, you are more likely to think of FedEx than U.S. Mail. If somebody asks for a Band-Aid or Kleenex, you know what they mean, even if you have an off-brand version. This association is the goal of every Hero Brand with its loyal customers and the broader consumer base.

Brands seek positive connections with users and non-users alike. Amazon appeals to the mainstream as a viable option to order and receive goods. Though I may not use the service, the company is always one of my options.

Switching Cost

Humans are generally creatures of habit, preferring the comfort of the status quo to the risk of change. This tendency – brand loyalty - is a strategic advantage for Hero Brands that dominate markets. Brand switching happens when a company's customer buys a product from a different brand than they usually prefer. Price is a primary consideration when introducing new products, especially when competing with an established product.

New brands or those new to a market segment typically overcome consumer reluctance to switch products by lowering the price of their recent entries. Established brands counter the low-price strategy by lowering the price of their products or amplifying the benefits of their products versus the new ones. The latter strategy's success depends on the established brand's ability to create a positive advantage in the customer's mind. If two products are viewed as the same – providing similar benefits – price is always the determining factor.

Toothpaste is a product typically indistinguishable from one brand to another. While I have a favorite brand (recommended by my dentist years ago), I will purchase an

alternative brand if my regular toothpaste is not on the shelf. When my toothpaste choice is available, I will only consider another brand *if* the price is abnormally low.

Companies strive to create products with a reservoir of mass appeal long before a consumer makes a purchase. When I lived in the United States, I preferred to buy American cars. When I moved to the Middle East, I intended to buy an American car. During my investigation, a Japanese carmaker offered a price discount on their automobiles, models I knew to be of high quality from their advertising over the years. I switched to the Japanese brand - advocating its benefits to friends and family – even as I maintained my emotional connection with American automobiles. If the Japanese brand had not generated mass appeal with features equivalent or superior to the American brands, I would have purchased the American alternative.

This scenario illustrates the advantage of an affiliation with a Hero Brand. Some consumers are willing to try an affiliated brand's product based on their positive connection with the Hero Brand.

Soft drinks are a great example of the power of connection. Coca-Cola and Pepsi are Hero Brands; each is regularly listed first in research polls as their followers' brand of soft drink choice. Surprisingly, those who prefer one brand to the other rarely have negative associations with the other brand. Quite a few have switched between the brands because of taste preferences.

Both brands have mass appeal, leading to a higher probability of gaining new customers when they try the product. Coca-Cola's CEO once said that Pepsi was the best thing that ever happened to Coca-Cola. It prevented a government charge of a Coca-Cola monopoly, led to the company developing a distinct public persona, and increased the global size of the soft drink market.

Keys to Mass Appeal

Accessibility, exposure, reputation, and consistent brand image are keys to achieving mass appeal. The technology industry provides examples of companies that are Hero Brands and those that have fallen from grace.

Sony PlayStation, Xbox, and Nintendo are Hero Brands in the gaming industry. While fans have loyalty to a specific gaming platform, the quality and appeal of particular game titles drive purchases. Consumers regularly switch consoles to play a new module without losing their affection for their brand or vilifying the competition.

Samsung and the iPhone are another example of Hero Brands sharing the Smartphone space without affecting their rival's image. Consumers may prefer one but are willing to use the other. For example, many people own both makes, a Samsung phone for personal use and an iPhone for business. Their comfort level with each model is evidence of their mutual appeal.

Mass appeal and likability are common themes with Hero Brands. If you see a fashionable coat hanging in the show window of a popular boutique store, it draws your eye. Whether it is your size, fits your body type, or is priced beyond your budget, you find the garment remarkable. Though you would never consider buying it, the coat's color and style attract you. Hero Brands exhibit similar mass appeal.

How do you identify mass appeal?

Everyone has different preferences. Is there a way to measure mass appeal that is more objective than intuitive or based on personal experience? One typical method is the top-of-mind index. A researcher might interview a consumer, or a consumer might fill out a survey with non-leading questions such as, "What are the first brands that come to your mind when you want to have a cup of coffee?" The response will tell you the mass appeal and the consumer's comfort level of a brand or several brands. In most cases, the answer includes the three leading brands in the industry.

For example, in questions about coffeehouses or baristas, Starbucks is among the top three responses, even when the interviewee does not regularly drink coffee. Similarly, Nike and Adidas brands are listed most frequently in surveys about sneakers.

Research of this type does not reflect the identity of a coveted loyal customer position but a broader view of the brand's perception generally. Social media research suggests the number of brand followers or interactions since a person only *likes* or *follows* a page if they have a positive image of the brand.

Some brands adapt the Balanced Scorecard (BCS) to evaluate brand loyalty by replacing operating metrics with metrics that include "top of mind" results, social media, brand posture, preference, value, perception, and referral rates. The scorecard facilitates the connection between the brand's market effectiveness to its financials and feeds its strategic planning.

Visual mapping data enables managers to locate the brand within the mass appeal spectrum and identify the Hero Brands and competitors. At least three themes of differentiation will emerge:

- **Distinct** as in luxury brands such as Rolex and Tiffany.

- **Limited** as in the fast-food (McDonald's, Burger King) or soft drink (Coca-Cola, Pepsi Cola) industries.

- **Minimal,** as in most household products

What are some important lessons learned about the mass appeal of brands?

A brand personality must be authentic and consistent. For example, a luxury brand with high prices naturally competes for a smaller target market. When luxury brands offer an economical product line, the brand image suffers because low price conflicts with their public personality.

The Rolex brand is synonymous with luxury, sophistication, and leadership. The Swiss company advertises its connection with sports and movie stars in luxurious locations. A model known as the "Rolex President" is named for the many United States Presidents who have worn it. Unsurprisingly, Rolex consistently rates high in "top-of-mind" surveys though few of the respondents own or intend to purchase one of its watches.

Luxury Hero Brands maintain their status through their mass appeal. They appear accessible to a broader audience than their loyal customers. Anybody can walk into a Rolex store and browse its products without fear of intimidation.

Customer service is a component of mass appeal, though the level of services expected varies with the brand. Few consumers expect the personal attention of a sales assistant in Harrod's of London or in a local Walmart. Nevertheless, the level of customer service must meet or exceed the customer's expectations in delivering a positive experience.

If customer service falters, the brand image fails as well. Everyone remembers a time when they received poor customer service. How did you feel about the brand immediately after? How long did that feeling persist? Has the company regained your trust?

Humility - modesty, respect for others, and thankfulness – is an appealing aspect of human and company personalities.

For decades, Sears maintained leadership in home goods, tools, appliances, and home improvement. They demonstrated respect for their customers through the quality and warranty of their products, especially Craftsman tools. As time passed, the company switched to inferior materials for their tools, confident that customers would overlook the quality decline and a shorter warranty. The reality of their products failed to equal their image in the public's mind. Feeling betrayed and disrespected, once loyal customers departed in droves for tools of better quality and price. The Craftsman line never recovered, nor did the Sears brand.

Hero Brands create an emotional connection between the brand and consumers. They understand the relationship only develops when their personality and promise are aligned. Authenticity is crucial. Nike is known for its slogan, "Just do it." This sentiment applies to more than athletes; it is a motivational concept relatable to everyone.

Are you nervous about a job interview? "Just do it." As babies learn to walk, we can see their efforts to "just do it."

Consumers often connect with multiple brands, sometimes using both without discrimination. When they switch from the first brand to the alternative, the reason is usually that the original brand fails to make a solid connection.

Hero Brands find out why their customers connect emotionally by asking them. They know that connection is only possible when consumers are comfortable and have good experiences with the brand.

Some brands unintentionally intimidate potential customers when they focus on less important aspects of the relationship. All luxury brands confront leakage – theft by employees and customers – and many overreact. Imagine going into a Louis Vuitton and an armed security guard watched you shop.

While some may discount security as necessary in troubled times, most of us feel intimidated when security staff follows us. The image we had entering the store vanishes, replaced by the memory of a hostile guard. The brand's personality becomes intimidating in the consumers' minds. A couple able to afford an exquisite meal at a fancy restaurant once a year wants a grand experience. They expect that some restaurants deliberately drive off customers who do not fit their desired type. When they find a restaurant with a welcoming staff, the couple will share their great experience through social media and friends.

Sometimes a brand can maintain quality but fails to innovate as consumers' tastes change, like the previous examples of Nokia and Boston Market. Even the best brands can stumble and struggle to keep up with trends. More people expect healthy food options, even at fast food restaurants. Kentucky Fried Chicken (KFC) has been a leading brand for years and is still high on the "top-of-mind" studies. However, they have struggled to connect to the younger generation emotionally.

Millennials expect meal options and are moving away from fried foods. Chick-fil-A, with almost 50% fewer restaurants and one less working day, has exceeded KFC's overall revenue in recent years. The gain occurred because Chick-fil-A understood the mass appeal of offering healthier and fresher food choices while being friendlier to consumers. As the founder of Chick-fil-A commented, **"Going the extra mile should be the second nature of all employees."**

Summary

Hero Brands garner mass appeal and maintain their target markets. The brand identity and, more importantly, personality remains authentic and consistent, setting the stage for a genuine emotional connection between the consumer and the brand.

Hero Brands treat their customers as family. They are humble, even if they are known as luxury brands. Innovation is continuous and mandatory. Heroes provide multiple opportunities for potential customers to try their products. The additional options make the brand accessible and create a bond with potential customers. If you target a niche market, stay humble and likable but do not turn your back on the rest of the market. You always know the source of your next loyal customer. My metaphor for mass appeal is: "don't be afraid to tell a joke if you are known to be serious; just be careful that you do not cross the line of being a clown". This is the difference between humility and humiliation. Brands are no different!

Trait 8: Proven Growth History

What is historical growth, and why is it important?

Historical growth is an essential factor in the overall health of a brand. There are multiple variations for determining historical growth, each with pros and cons. Hero brands demonstrate stable and continued growth, while innovative brands on the verge of Hero status show similar trends of shorter durations.

Hero Brands are the best of the best. They do not begin with the largest market share or a loyal following. Many, like Amazon, begin unknown and untested and carefully implement the strategies herein to become best-in-class disruptors. Amazon's brand status reflected its growth as it dominated the online retail industry. Increasing revenues follow a brand's creation and successful appeal to a customer base. Consistent growth in the customer base indicates that the brand has sufficient mass appeal and personality to keep developing.

Other traits, such as filling a gap in the market or its ability to adapt to changing customer requirements, position the brand to grow naturally. Apple's international success requires loyal customers and a steady influx of new customers. Apple's ability to anticipate what potential customers want spurs their foreign and domestic growth.

Hero Brands proactively strategize growth rather than passively waiting for it to occur. They become so attuned to the market that they grow naturally.

What to look for?

"**Go where you grow; don't grow as you go**" is my favorite saying. When a brand's growth exceeds its ability to deliver its promise or conflicts with customer needs, customers leave, market share drops, and brand equity suffers.

Hero Brands maintain demand by developing a loyal customer base on a local, regional, or international scale. A single cookie-cutter approach to customer growth does not exist; each Hero Brand follows a slightly different, sometimes unique, strategy for developing its customer base.

KIA

The company began in 1944 in South Korea as bicycle and steel tube manufacturer, then expanding into manufacturing Honda motorcycles in 1957 then expanded to Mazda trucks in 1962. They began manufacturing Mazda and Fiat automobiles in 1973. In 1992, the company opened four Kia dealerships in Portland, Oregon before expanding to 100 dealerships in 30 American states in 1995. After bankruptcy in 1997, Hyundai, another South Korean auto manufacturer, acquired 51% control of Kia.

Kia's progress is like the journey of Japanese auto company Honda. Both companies gradually built their expertise with smaller-sized economy automobiles in the Asian Market before expanding to the United States, Europe, and globally. In each expansion to a new market, the companies featured low-priced models of dubious quality to gain a foothold before scaling upward with in-country manufacturing plants (Philippines, Vietnam, Slovakia, China, United States, and Mexico), larger upscale models with superior workmanship and quality. Edmunds ranks Kia vehicles among the top finishers in expert ratings. The number of Kia units sold globally in 2020 was over 2.6 million, an increase of 58% in ten years.

Many Hero brands like KIA have employed a step-by-step growth strategy, entering markets serially from local to regional to national to international. Some brands bypass a step, starting locally, expanding regionally, then jumping to global markets. Some brands employ their expansion strategy to individual products, each growing at its own pace.

McDonald's

Success begets success. The growth of the fast-food chain has endured for years based on a consistent, low-priced version of the prototypical American hamburger. For many people worldwide, the brand and its Golden Arches are synonymous with the American spirit and culture. The company, which has been around for generations, is still growing, with over 38,000 locations in 100 countries. The brand is an international behemoth.

The Importance of Domestic Growth

In 2015, a Swedish consultant approached me to introduce the owner of a new café brand who wanted to expand to Dubai, where economic growth was booming.

After the introduction, I met the owner, who eagerly explained the brand's history and authenticity. He went into great detail about its differentiating factors, claiming each to be a unique feature that potential competitors lacked. He insisted that brand identification was strong, having been in business for 15 years, and was positive nothing like it existed in Dubai. In his mind, the lack of competitive venues practically guaranteed a successful market opening. The excited owner was obviously proud of his brand.

When I inquired about locations in other countries, he replied, "None. I've just been waiting for the right opportunity, and I think Dubai is it."

"How many locations do you have in Sweden?" I asked.

"One," he replied.

A little stunned, I asked, "Why did you choose Dubai to expand? Why haven't you expanded in your backyard after 15 years?"

The owner did not respond. I continued, "Growth in your own country—your backyard—is easiest because you live there and understand the culture, the market, and the competition. The vital information - things you don't know about other countries - is available to you. If you can't grow at home, why do you think you can grow in Dubai?"

He stared at me, a frown on his face. Our discussion was over. In hindsight, it was one of my shortest meetings ever.

The Importance of Growth Trends versus One-Year Wonders

In addition to the number of units, year-to-year total revenue growth is essential. Relying on a single year or a short-term period can be misleading due to abnormal fluctuations. For example, if investors only considered a restaurant's income during the Covid restrictions, there would be no new investments in that industry.

A Hero Brand constantly adapts to changing circumstances. Sometimes, the consequences include shutting down operations in one country and expanding in others. In other cases, a company might reinvest in existing locations while delaying new openings.

Tim Hortons

Tim Hortons, Canada largest quick-service restaurant chain, was founded in 1964 by a hockey player, merged with Wendy's Restaurants in 1995, and became publicly traded in 2006. In 2014, Burger King acquired the company. Rapidly expanding since the acquisition, the company has more than 5,300 stores in 16 countries, including more than 300 in the Middle East, over 500 in the US, and 1000 in China.

The restaurant has been the fastest growing concept in the Middle East for the past two years, the number of units expected to double by 2028. Because of the heritage of the brand in Canada, Middle Eastern customers are already connected to the brand since many either lived or studied in Canada. The brand's growth from one cafe in 1964 to almost 3000 in Canada today indicates its growth potential as the brand emphasizes global expansion.

Starbucks

Starbucks's growth strategy resembles more of a series of shotgun blasts than other chains' typical rifle shot approach. They quickly dominate a market by rapidly opening multiple locations close to each other, avoiding store-to-store competition by expanding the total coffee-drinking customer base. Starbucks locations grew more than 350% from 2003 to 2020. During the same period, store growth in China, the company's second-largest market, was more than 2400% to almost 5000 locations in 2020.

Starbucks is a Hero Brand that disrupted the traditional coffee-drinking model, becoming a status symbol and a preferred destination. With the advantage of franchise financing, the company is a model of sustained mushroom growth.

Carrefour French Hypermarket

Some Hero brands deliberately limit growth due to their conservative culture, a characteristic many consider a weakness. An external event like a merger, divestiture, or change in control ignites a willingness to risk expansion. Carrefour French Hypermarket went from a local French brand to a European brand. It became a global brand by merging with Majid Al Futtaim (MAF) Group in the Middle East. With prodding from MAF, the brand expanded to the Middle East, increased its store locations, and evolved into an iconic brand with a solid equity base. Sometimes a brand grows steadily but at a slower pace than its competitors. Don't overlook brands with lower growth if it remains steadily upward. An unexpected event can suddenly boost its trajectory.

Market Disrupters

Hero brands in the technology industry are rare since maintaining a dominant share for an extended period is difficult. Technological advances occur so rapidly that traditional competitor barriers - patents, copyrights, unique features - no longer exist. A list of former industry leaders includes Blockbusters, Compaq, AltaVista, and AOL. Many were first to market and enjoyed brief periods of revenue and profit growth, only to fall victim to a newer, better, or cheaper supplier of a similar product. The adage "Those who live by the sword die by the sword" is valid for technology companies.

Historical growth is limited in the industry because new advances supplant new companies' products or one of the Hero brands acquires the smaller disrupting company (one of the reasons a company becomes a Hero brand). Companies like Apple, Google, Microsoft, and Amazon, with a few others, are Hero brands because they have sustained excellence and industry domination for years of growth.

Comparing companies' long-term growth helps distinguish between potential Hero brands and also-rains. A competitive comparison, product by product, region to region, or year to year, highlights companies with low growth or pursuing unsustainable growth relative to their competitors.

Single Product Hero Brands

While most Hero Brands offer multiple products (Amazon or Apple), some reach Hero status with a single product. The Louisville Slugger company has produced only wooden baseball bats for generations worldwide. Separating the bat from the sport is almost impossible. Movie brands like MGM, Paramount, and Walt Disney are instantly recognized by every moviegoer anywhere movies are available. Hero brands are not tied to a single country or ethnicity.

Summary

The nine traits described in this book are interconnected and complementary and based on universal principles:

1. A Brand's personality draws in the customer.
2. Mass appeal and the desirable loyal customer base leads to profitability.
3. Profitability is mandatory for investment.

4. Growth is only possible with adequate investment for expansion.

Hero brands excel in these principles. Walmart is a Hero Brand known for its phenomenal growth. - 28.76% growth in United States stores between 2008 and 2017 - even during economic downturns. The company's multiple store designs are familiar in communities worldwide.

The growth of a brand is the story of its success, ability to identify the right markets, satisfy multiple demands, and capture mass appeal. Some brands discover the formula for local growth but founder when they expand regionally or globally. Their inability arises from a lack of international experience, an inadequate support system, supply chain expertise, or unique product specifications, each crucial for the growth of a brand.

There are many examples of brands that grew too fast and fizzled out before they reached Hero status. Not all business models meet the requirements of a Hero Brand. Remember, if someone approaches to franchise a brand internationally, review several years of revenue growth to determine if it is growing, declining, or stagnant. If a brand can't succeed at home, it's unlikely to grow anywhere!

Trait 9: Innovative

Innovation is one of the prerequisites that ignites a brand and drives sales. Some say that it infuses a company's culture and inspires leadership. Hero Brands continuously innovate. Innovation is more than new products or traditional research; it enables a brand to discover fresh perspectives and constantly improve. Innovation propels brands to market dominance by expanding opportunities in new markets.

Hero Brands - Apple, Microsoft, Tesla, Rolex, and McDonald's - stay on the offensive to remain leaders in their industries.

Companies utilize multiple strategies to maintain an innovation lead, including:

- **Breakthrough:** Developing new products that revolutionize people's work and play is a proven strategy to maintain superiority. iRobot introduced the Roomba in 2002, the first robotic vacuum sweeper that replaced hours of manual labor. The company continued to improve its product over the years and dominates the market today. The sophisticated use of technology is persistent with Hero Brands.

- **Open:** Adding new twists to old proprietary and competitive products is widely practiced among Hero brands. Successful products always attract imitations. With just enough difference to avoid patent protection, a dominant brand can quickly gain significant market share with less risk and greater profits through its size and established customer base. Despite Amazon's head start in online marketing, Walmart's online sales rival its competitor.

- **Incremental:** Constant innovation through small changes to existing products is a competitive barrier. Apple and its practice of minor improvements in its iPhone Brands keep would-be industry challengers on their heels.

- **Disruptive:** A product or service that disrupts an industry is the goal of every company. Disruption occurs when a company creates a new brand or product to fill an unknown or impossible-to-solve need. Disruptive brands develop new markets and tend to dominate them for years. Amazon and Meta (Facebook) practically invented eCommerce and social media and continue to dominate.

- **Reverse:** Hero brands develop skills to "reverse engineer" - identifying, analyzing, and re-configuring competitive products - and then adopt them.

Domino's Pizza changed its order and delivery process by exploiting social media channels. After implementing online ordering with an interactive tracking system, the company used Twitter with emojis of pizza slices as a channel to receive orders. Combining online ordering through social media increased Domino's market share to 13%. It transformed the company from one step behind its competition to leading the pack. The company started to position itself as an IT company selling pizza like McDonald's when its CEO described it as Real Estate company selling burger. If you invested ten thousand dollars in Domino's stock in 2012, you would've been a millionaire. It is simply because of the disruption the brand created through innovation.

Increased market share is a frequent side effect of successful innovation. Amazon broke the retail mold by introducing online-only stores when consumers were limited to brick-and-mortar retail locations.

Hero brands understand their market and customer base. By using methods in this book, they consistently innovate and deliver exceptional customer experiences.

Innovate or die by implementing efficient systems that meet and exceed customer expectations. The following metrics provide a window into a brand's stance on innovation.

Benchmark vs. Competition

Measuring their performance versus the competition enables Hero brands to remain in the lead and identify changing consumer preferences. Toyota tracks its internal processes for comparison to the past and its competitors. Since other automotive brands often adopt the company's innovative processes, Toyota must continually improve to maintain its advantage.

New ideas or methods must be reproducible to scale to a brand-wide level. Creating a benchmark indicates that the process is repeatable and measurable.

Customer Satisfaction

Customer satisfaction studies provide insight into the strengths and weaknesses of a brand. Hero brands target an exceptional, repeatable customer experience. Walmart's game-changing inventory system raised customer expectations for product availability. Similarly, Prime, Amazon's subscription-based shopping service, changed standards for convenience and delivery. Not too long ago, customers waited four to six weeks for a mail-order product, never considering delivery within the same day. The convenience of shopping at home with rapid delivery challenged the benefits of brick-and-mortar retailing.

Hero brands continually raise and meet customer expectations so that the company's customer experience becomes unique; potential customers don't consider other alternatives.

Apple is a master of this strategy. Before people stop talking about their latest product, the company introduces a new and improved version. Their customers rarely consider a purchase of other brands. When a brand reaches this status, it is at the top of its game.

On the other hand, some companies lag the technology curve, losing market share year after year to more sophisticated competitors. Blackberry, once the leader in personal online communication, has been in a catch-up mode for years. They failed to realize that customers are loyal to tomorrow's products, not yesterday's offerings. I was a die-hard Blackberry user for years. Eventually, I switched to other brands to meet today's business demands. A Hero brand is never satisfied with the status quo, even if its customers are.

Speed of Service (or Process)

The effects of innovative processes, such as an improvement in the speed of service, are measurable. How long does it take to deliver new stock to a location? How long does it take to fulfill an order? Hilton tracks the time between room turnover and the quarters' cleanliness level. McDonald's tracks order fulfillment time, i.e., the time between ordering and receiving food. Fabrication companies record downtimes and production rates. Microsoft and Apple measure customer service calls' response, duration, and results.

Online Sales vs. Store Sales

An innovative process - offering online sales - can be measured by the ratio of online sales to store sales. Amazon researched how customers used their service and added same-day delivery and small "grab and go" stores. Automobile retailers improved their customer experience by offering online shopping. Companies like Carvana and Autobahn Motors responded by offering virtual vending machines with online purchases and direct delivery to buyers so that a physical location is optional. Buying a car without spending the day at a dealership was not possible as little as ten years ago.

Employee Satisfaction

Innovative companies recognize the importance of creativity and empower employees to recommend improvements. Hero brands tend to have higher employee satisfaction, super-charging employee recruitment. People want to be part of a growing company that invests in employees. Innovation is more than cutting costs or downsizing. Unsurprisingly, Hero brands tend to downsize the least. Numerous companies cut employees without realizing the negative impact on customer service, trading a long-term asset (image) for short-term cost savings.

Cost Efficiency Connected to the New Technology or Innovation

improvements that matter to the customer is the intent of implementing innovative processes or using new technology. Sometimes, a combination of measures is necessary to capture a change's effects. For example, learning to read a page more quickly is futile if reading comprehension goes down simultaneously.

Profitability is an excellent indicator of the efficiency of innovation. Many companies fall into the productivity paradox, implementing innovative ideas without improving the bottom line. Investing in innovation and new technology is positive when the impact on the brand is positive.

Market Share Gain

Growth in market share for the organization (Domino's Pizza) or individual products (Samsung) indicates a brand's health. Being able to identify stagnation or loss of market share is vital. Failing to innovate is a sure path to obsolescence.

Kodak, once the dominant company in the photography industry, overlooked the industry's digital evolution. Its persistence with physical images enabled other brands to become leaders in the digital market. Over time, digital imagery replaced Kodak's traditional film market. Brands cannot successfully innovate as an occasional or intermittent strategy. Innovation is a process embedded in a company's culture.

Polaroid made the same mistakes. Digital photography with revolutionary editing features replaced the company's instant photo technology. Polaroid responded by rebranding its cameras. While sales improved, their cameras remain a novelty rather than a market leader.

Successful innovation is linked to the consumer and remains faithful to the brand identity. Technological advances typically affect consumer demand and a brand's internal processes simultaneously. The introduction of smartphones and the appearance of new applications disrupted the communication industry. The mobile version of a traditional telephone became a minicomputer accessible to everybody. Job functions previously tethered to a physical office were possible anywhere with a reliable internet connection. Overnight, companies could remotely recruit, hire, train, and manage employees. Virtual office visits and real-time online conversations replaced expensive, time-consuming travel. Hero brands learned to measure technology effectiveness by its impact on customer satisfaction, revenue growth, and adoption rates.

Determining the length of a technical lifecycle - the time remaining before the next innovation or disruption supplants the technology - is challenging for all companies. Smartphones enjoyed explosive growth for over a decade until most brands offered similar capabilities.

Hero Brands learn to anticipate future transformation and consumer reactions to deliver a new feature before demand has materialized. They accept the risks of making the wrong choice, overstaying a market, or moving too quickly. They understand that timing and agility are critical.

Toys "R" Us Story

As I prepared to publish the first issue of this book, another sad story about the principle of "innovate or die" came to mind. Like many Americans, I was shocked when Toys "R" Us filed for bankruptcy. For years, the toy store giant dominated the retail toy industry, bringing joy to millions of children each year. Investors generally consider companies like Toys "R" Us invulnerable to bankruptcy since the link between children and toys is perpetual and eternal.

The dot-com industry was booming in 1999, and Toys "R" Us was a significant beneficiary of online shopping fervor. The company's website was overwhelmed during that Christmas season with orders to be shipped before Christmas. Delivery schedules were lengthened, and many buyers did not receive their orders on time. After being fined $350,000 by the US Federal Trade Commission, the company invested $60 million to support its online business and become Amazon's exclusive toy supplier.

The partnership with Amazon enabled Toy "R" Us to become the world's top online toy seller. Recognizing an opportunity, Amazon extended its platform to other retailers selling toys unavailable through Toys "R" Us. Management at Toys "R" Us protested the new competition.

Consequently, Amazon's CEO offered Toys "R" Us exclusivity if it would extend its product range to include toys like those sold by other companies on the Amazon site.

Toys "R" Us sued Amazon for breach of contract, leading to a five-year court battle. Ultimately, Amazon paid Toys "R" Us $51 million and ended the sales partnership.

Toys "R" Us prevailed in the lawsuit at the cost of its association with the world's #1 online sales company. Amazon sales subsequently exploded, soaring from $2.78

billion in 2000 to \$136 billion in 2017. During the same period, Toys "R" Us revenues were stagnant - about \$11 billion annually — while debt grew to \$5 billion, forcing the company to file for bankruptcy.

The difference between the two companies was their mindset and willingness to change. If Toys "R" Us had been more insightful, agreeing to collaborate with Amazon, it would have likely continued to be the number one toy seller in the world.

I cannot find a better synopsis of this story or innovation than Amazon's CEO Jeff Bezos' quote:

"We have had three big ideas in Amazon that we've stuck with for eighteen years, and they are the reason we are successful: put the customer first, invent, and be patient. What we need to do is always lean into the future; when the world changes around you and when it changes against you, you have to lean into that and figure out what to do because complaining isn't a strategy."

Summary

Hero brands constantly evolve and innovate. Their mantra is "Innovate or die." They recognize that timing is everything. A brand must be early enough to recover initial costs and be able to convince customers they need the innovative product. If a brand is too late, they lose market share and must play catch-up to the new leader.

Technology is a tool that is used to enhance innovative processes. Technology keeps the brand alive while innovation moves it ahead.

Conclusion

We have been on the journey of discovering what makes a Hero Brand different, which becomes apparent from the initial approach throughout the lifecycle of a brand. Hero Brands look beyond discovering what a market needs but focuses on what the customer needs, or if there is a customer need within the market gap. They create an experience, and loyal customers develop based on that experience rather than the product itself. Then, products or services are created to meet those needs rather than trying to create customers for a developed product or service. Hero Brands create the demand or go where the demand is already in existence.

Hero Brands continually adapt based on their customers' changing needs, which leads to a strengthened longevity of a brand. They remain relevant over time. Remember that people buy brands and devour products. Investing in a Hero Brand means investing in the demand created by that brand. They understand and effectively maintain that demand throughout their lifetime. I am a believer that customers give permission for a brand to grow. Without it, the brand becomes stagnates. Hero Brands remain open and accessible to potential new customers without intimidating them or without losing appreciation for their loyal customers. They live by constant innovation because it is either innovate or die.

A Hero Brand will fill a need while never abandoning its personality. To build a loyal customer base, personality means everything. Personality is what enables the emotional connection required to turn a consumer into a loyal customer. Brands without a strong and distinct personality become lost in the ether, never to return to the top of a customer's mind. Timing is everything. Hero Brands enter the market with the right personality at the right time. Being too early or too late can be costly.

The personality of a Hero does not conflict with various cultures when they grow globally. Rather, they embrace the local culture without abandoning their personality that made them a success in the first place. Therefore, it is imperative for a Hero Brand to be rated PG, so it can accommodate any culture when it eventually expands globally or as I call it *'the glocalization factor"*. The idea of globalization should start from the principle that "one size does not fit all" when it comes to growth. Heroes offer options that can be successful in any location, based on available real estate or market needs. They maintain their brand regardless if they are in a small space, a massive complex or online. In fact, sometimes it is better to go smaller for a better ROI to allow greater saturation when it enters a new area. Some brands make the mistake of growing at an unsustainable rate. The other side is just as serious of an issue. If a brand cannot grow locally where success is leaning toward its favor, then a brand cannot be successful globally.

Investing in a brand incorporates some risk, but it is greatly reduced in a Hero Brand with their record of accomplishing the right things at the right time. Hero Brands invariably implement exceptional processes and methods to become the superstars of their market. Operational excellence is more than a bullet point in their annual report or marketing plan. They understand that profitability is what keeps a brand going and are not afraid to invest strategically. Heroes take it one step further by leading their market in profitability. They anticipate and plan for growth as an inherent part of their planning. Heroes don't shy away from technology or innovation. Technology keeps a brand relevant, and innovation propels them to Hero status, but they avoid the productivity paradox and focus on innovation that leads to greater profitability. In order to be a global superstar, a Hero Brand incorporated scalability into their model. This allows them to adapt to where their customers need them, whether it is a small location or massive complex.

In my 28 years working with top Hero Brands, and others that are far from being Heroes, I realized the difference a Hero Brand can do to an organization or an investor. Companies that foster or invest in Hero Brands create a safety net when things get tough, while companies that rely on unheroic ones collapse rather quickly.

The intention of this book is to save entrepreneurs and small investors from falling into the trap of brands that may look good but will not redeem their investments. I have witnessed both. I worked for organizations where brands were chosen because the owner or the CEO had a good personal experience or preference. I even worked for organizations where brands were franchised because both CEOs are friends and thought they should collaborate. I have seen all of them collapse and did not go beyond the first location. I came up with the HERO adjective believing that brands should be saviors to their companies, and they should be there to last and prosper. They should worry about you rather you worry about them in difficult times.

Before publishing the book, I provided the manuscript to my friends and colleagues to read and give feedback, they returned with the following questions:

- What if the brand is missing one or two traits, should we consider it a Hero?
- Is there a quantitative model to measure the Hero status?
- Can a new brand reach the Hero status from the start?
- Can you call Nokia, Kodak, and Sears Hero brands at the time they were flourishing? What if you had invested in them at that time, how do you know when to exit?

I mentioned in the introduction that the nine traits are debatable, and some may think there are more or less to achieve the Hero status. I had no intentions to create a quantitative model for people to use; instead, I wanted to create a reference whenever someone is confused about a brand and its viability to invest, buy, or franchise. In my opinion, a brand must achieve all nine traits before giving it the Hero status. You may call some brands promising, great, profitable, or successful but until you check all the boxes for the nine traits, you cannot award them the Hero status.

It is difficult for a brand to be a Hero after its debut. There are traits that are difficult to measure at the time of the introduction such as growth history, its value, and its mass appeal even if it satisfies other traits. You may plan strategically, and you introduce a homegrown brand to the market; however, you must take into consideration all nine traits when introducing such a brand. Additionally, indeed, Nokia, Kodak and Sears were once Heroes. Their inability to see the speed of change and their lack of urgency to innovate made them irrelevant and obsolete to today's consumers. The nine traits are almost like a connected puzzle. Some traits like innovation are vital, once the brand loses it, it loses the status of being Hero. We have been seeing signs of comeback by Nokia in the last few years with new smart phones; however, the brand turned from being a market leader to a market follower to survive. There are signs that the brand is falling behind, such as market share, profitability, and geographical growth, but the health of any business or any brand is the same store growth or like-for-like growth. If the existing business is growing year over year without extra channels for sales, it is a great sign that there is a demand, and the brand is flourishing. The number of viewers for TV shows is the main indicator for whether to continue or withdraw any particular show; it is the same for any brand.

Therefore, if you are an entrepreneur, investor or someone who wants to work for a solid brand, do your homework and use these nine traits to evaluate the brand you will invest in or work for. Hero Brands give you a sense of security, and their equity represents your needed safety net.

These nine traits have been invaluable both personally and professionally. Take these nine traits and make them your own. I want to hear from you about how you used this book, what resonated with you, your success stories, and to answer any questions.

Thank you for reading!

Hesham Almekkawi

About the Author

Hesham Almekkawi is a Food and Beverage industry expert and international business leader with more than 28 years of experience in managing global and international chains of restaurants in the USA and the Middle East. He was appointed in 2021 as the CEO of AG Café International Management Company to spreadhead an aggressive growth plan for Tim Hortons in the Middle East. He is the founder of ATK Consulting in the United States and Ahramiz FZ LLC, a leadership development and management consulting company based in Dubai.

Prior to Tim Hortons, Hesham held several leadership positions for several conglomerate companies. He was the Vice President of Hospitality for Majid Al Futtaim Group and, the Chief Operating Officer for Kuwait Food Company (Americana) in UAE.

Prior moving to Dubai in 2008, Mr. Almekkawi was the Regional Director of Pizza Hut for the Mid-Atlantic Region in the United States where he spent 13 years with YUM! Brands.

Mr. Almekkawi holds EMBA from the Zicklin School of Business in New York, where he served afterword as an adjunct professor from 2003 to 2006 teaching service strategies and operations management.

Among his credentials, Mr. Almekkawi is a Certified International Life Coach, NLP Practitioner and Certified Public Speaker, Mentor and Coach by John Maxwell.

In 2023, he was chosen as one of the 200 global inspirational leaders by White Page International and one of the revolutionary global CEOs by CIOlook magazine. He was selected by Image RetailME as one of 100 Food and Beverage ICONS in 2023.

www.heshamalmekkawi.com

Quotes from the Author

"Customers purchase brands, and they consume products."

"Trusting a brand by definition comes within time after a long history of the brand delivering on its promises to consumers."

"When customers become engaged and connected, they elevate the brand."

"Filling the gap is not about how fast or how well a brand fulfills the need in that gap; it is about how different it will be from the other brands in order to become better and last longer."

"Being first to fill the market within the gap is not enough, the brand has to maintain its leadership position over time."

"Customers will not flock to a brand unless that brand offers something different, unique, and relevant."

"The lack of competition on the market map suggests the area needs further study."

"Do your homework—that's called research. It is better to spend a little money ahead instead of losing big later on."

"Hero Brands are made to last, and the first step to lasting is to proactively stay one step ahead of competition."

"Start first to last longer or start different to be better. Create a product for the customer or create a need for a product, but never try to create a customer for a product."

"The goal of developing a brand personality is to engage consumers so they create an emotional connection that will pave the path toward the coveted customer loyalty."

"Brand personality is not limited to traditional character traits but can include demographic data such as age or gender."

"Hero Brands have developed a way to remain relevant and connected to their consumers. They understand that personality creates the connections and character traits will keep the relationship going."

"An emotional connection with a brand is about how the brand makes you feel and how you relate to it."

"Changing a brand positioning to gain more customers can be fatal."

"Personality is the intangible equity of the brand. Never lose it or you will lose the brand itself."

"Brands should embrace the evolutions, not the revolutions."

"Hero Brands never change who they are for short-term gain. They design their marketing strategy for growth, not for revenue."

"The idea of *total experience* has become the norm for customer engagement nowadays."

"The game of customer experience is about the other complementary things which make the customer experience unique, uberised, cool, and instagrammable."

"Global brands embrace local and regional differences rather than a *one-size-fits-all* approach."

"Hero Brands are like chameleons. They are flexible enough and in tune with their customers to ensure their tastes, habits, values, religious beliefs, language, and local regulations are met without compromising the brand reputation."

"The first step in going global is to understand the internal and external challenges of the targeted market and how well and quickly the brand can adjust to meet these challenges."

"Global friendly brands prioritize local consumer habits. They are not trying to simply sell products but to become a part of a customer's routine for life."

"Hero Brands are not trying to simply sell products but to become a part of a customer's routine for life."

"Personnel that come from the local community will be able to gauge the changes and position the Hero Brand accordingly."

"Global friendly brand acceptance is culturally driven. Hero Brands are flexible and adapt to language barriers, customs, tastes, and regulations while maintaining the personality and positioning of the brand."

"Religious norms can make or break a brand's success."

"Hero brands adapt to the established language nuances and social norms."

"Unless you have a strong system in place, it is extremely difficult to control human behavior of the organization."

"I define operations as a system with a human touch that creates the connection with the consumer."

"Hero Brands understand that the human factor is key for the success of the organization. Instead of looking for the best doer, search for leadership traits and a collaborative attitude."

"Hero Brands understand the need to develop local suppliers that can provide the same quality of the homemade raw materials."

"Inventory is a necessary evil. Keep it low and keep it controlled."

"Hero Brands differentiate themselves by building the supply chain locally in the destination region before they go global. Supply local before you go global."

"A Hero Brand excels in operations by retaining its loyal and most experienced employees."

"Control labor cost but, never burn the furniture!"

"Create a system that captures the brand personality and let it operates."

"It is the customer's connection that sells, not the displayed high-resolution picture."

"In certain cases, the ability of the brand to have different prototypes is the only possible way to grow globally and become scalable."

"This is what Hero Brands do well. They never lose the identity, personality, or the positioning of the brand when they switch from one prototype to another."

"The scalability factor of a Hero Brand means it will thrive during the worst of economic times, have both mass appeal and a niche customer, and maintain the same brand identity."

"Growth is the health of the business and the fuel needed to increase overall profitability, which consequently, increases a company's market share."

"A brand will not reach Hero status if it focuses only on short-term revenues. Strategic planning and long-term marketing strategy are what differentiates a Hero Brand from other brands."

"Take care of people first and sales and profit will follow."

"You will have to earn the trust of your shareholders, customers, and employees. Lead by example."

"Reactivity means a brand loses focus on the future because it is busy putting out fires. They "repair" instead of 'prepare.'"

"Strategic planning is critical as a general guide of where a company wants to be in the future while keeping the end in mind."

"Many brands get satisfied having profit growth over the last year, but only a few looks at the lost opportunity and ask why there is not more."

"Hero Brands create a value system that does not compromise on the brand positioning nor the brand profitability."

"Invest in your employees and treat them as an invaluable part of the brand. They are the ones to deliver the brand promises to your customers."

"Accessibility, exposure, reputation, and consistent brand image are keys to achieving mass appeal."

"A person is not going to *like* or *follow* a page if they have a negative image of the brand."

"If customer service falters, then the brand image will fall as well."

"Hero Brands find out why their customers are connecting emotionally."

"If a consumer develops a connection with another brand, they may not abandon the first brand but may become a dual user. They may switch between brands easier than if the connection had never developed."

"Go where you grow; don't grow as you go."

"Some brands want to stay in a limited market, but most Hero Brands are international behemoths."

"Growth is not possible without the customer following and investment required for expansion."

"No brand will grow unless it finds the right market, right demand, and has enough mass appeal."

"If a brand can't grow at home, it can't grow anywhere!"

"Innovation is a process that enables a brand to find a fresh perspective in order to capture continuous improvement."

"Brands do not innovate for the sake of delivering something new or fresh. They implement efficient systems that will deliver on customer expectations or introduce new expectations that consumers had not thought of before."

"Impress your customers to the point that they don't think of anyone else."

"Hero Brands are never satisfied with today's offering, even if their customers are."

"Innovative companies inherently endorse creativity and empower employees to actively be involved with recommending improvements."

"Innovation is a process and culture. It is not something a brand can do occasionally under the pressure of losing customers and market share."

"Innovation must be linked to the consumer and remain true to the brand identity."

"Technology keeps the brand alive while innovation moves it ahead."

"A Hero Brand will fill a need while never abandoning its personality."

Bibliography

Aashish. (2016, September 10). "What is brand positioning? How to create a strong brand positioning strategy?" *Feedough.* Retrieved from https://www.feedough.com/brand-positioning/

Acclaro. (2016, September 7). "Globalization: Translating Your Marketing to Best Communicate Your Brand." [Web log comment]. Retrieved from http://www.acclaro.com/blog/globalization-translating-marketing-best-communicate-brand/

Adidas. (2016). "Adidas Annual Report." [PDF document]. Retrieved from http://www.adidas-group.com/media/filer_public/a3/fb/a3fb7068-c556-4a24-8eea-cc00951a1061/2016_eng_gb.pdf

Al-Hyari, K., Alnsour, M., Al-Weshah, G., & Haffar, M. (2012, June). "Religious Beliefs and Consumer Behaviour: From loyalty to boycotts." *Journal of Islamic Marketing,* 3(2), 155-174. DOI 10.1108/17590831211232564.

Almekkawi, H. (2016, November 29). "What does a 'HERO' F&B brand look like?" Retrieved from https://www.linkedin.com/

Anderson, M., Anderson, E.J., & Parker, G. (n.d.). "Why Operations Management if Important for Your Company."

Operations Management for Dummies. Retrieved from http://www.dummies.com/business/operations-management/why-operations-management-is-important-for-your-company/

Beach, A., & Kaboolian, L. (n.d.). "Working Better Together: A Practical Guide for Union Leaders, Elected Officials and Managers to Improve Public Services." [PDF document]. Retrieved from http://www.law.harvard.edu/programs/lwp/Working%20Better%20Together.pdf

Blanchet, J., Arvor, S., Fitoussi, B., Laboureur, G., et al. (2013, October). "A Journey to Operational Excellence." *The Capco Institute Journal of Financial Transformation*. Retrieved from http://www.capco.com/insights/capco-institute/a-journey-to-operational-excellence

Blecker, T., Kersten, W., & Ringle, C.M. (2015, August). "Operational Excellence in Logistics and Supply Chains: Optimization Methods, Data-driven Approaches and Security Highlights." *Hamburg International Conference of Logistics*. Vol 22. [PDF document]. Retrieved from https://hicl.org/publications/2015/22/1.pdf

Brand Personality. (n.d.). In *Investopedia*. Retrieved from http://www.investopedia.com/terms/b/brand-personality.asp?partner=asksa

Brooks, C. (2013, September 13). "Innovation: Key to Successful Business." *Business News Daily*. Retrieved from http://www.businessnewsdaily.com/5167-innovation.html

Brown, M. (n.d.). "Why You Need to Measure Brand Equity – And How Do I Do It?" *Kissmetrics*. [Web log content]. Retrieved https://blog.kissmetrics.com/measure-brand-equity/

Buelow, D.M. (n.d.). "12 Mistakes to avoid in Site Selection." *Deloitte*. [PDF document]. Retrieved from https://www2.deloitte.com/content/dam/Deloitte/us/Documents/process-and-operations/us-cons-siteselection-12-mistakes-120110.pdf

Caan, J. (2013, October 24). "How to Spot a Gap in the Market." Retrieved from https://www.linkedin.com/pulse/20131024123736-32175171-how-to-spot-a-gap-in-the-market

Camhi, J. (2014, June 24). "5 Tools to Identify Gaps in Your Customer Experience Strategy." *InformationWeek, Bank Systems & Technology*. Retrieved from http://www.banktech.com/management-strategies/5-tools-to-identify-gaps-in-your-customer-experience-strategy/d/d-id/1297077?

Carrefour. (2015). "Registration Document: 2015 Annual Report." [PDF Document]. Retrieved from http://www.carrefour.com/sites/default/files/carrefourregistration_document_2015_annual_financial_report.pdf

Castaldo, J. (n.d.). "The Last Days of Target." *Canadian Business*. Retrieved from http://www.canadianbusiness.com/the-last-days-of-target-canada/

Charan, R. & Lafley, A.G. (2008, May 30). "Why Innovation Matters." *Fast Company*. Retrieved at https://www.fastcompany.com/874798/why-innovation-matters

Chaudhuri, S. (2007, July 24). "Lost in Translation: How Do Linguistic Differences Affect Global Marketing." *Fast Company*. [Web log content]. Retrieved from https://www.fastcompany.com/679197/lost-translation-how-do-linguistic-differences-affect-global-marketing

Clark, L. (2013, October 19). "Founders to Young Entrepreneurs: 'Find a gap in the market and own that problem'." Wired. Retrieved from http://www.wired.co.uk/article/young-entrepreneurs

Costa, J. (2014, September 22). "Innovate or Die: Why Innovation Matters." *Huffington Post*. Retrieved from http://www.huffingtonpost.com/jose-costa/innovate-or-die-why-innov_b_5610832.html

Dahlhoff, D. (2015, January 20). "Why Target's Canadian Expansion Failed." *Harvard Business Review*. Retrieved from https://hbr.org/2015/01/why-targets-canadian-expansion-failed

D'Aveni, R.A. (2007, November). "Mapping Your Competitive Positions." *Harvard Business Review*. Retrieved from https://hbr.org/2007/11/mapping-your-competitive-position

Dawar, N. & Bagga, C.K. (2015 June). "A Better Way to Map Brand Strategy." *Harvard Business Review.* Retrieved from https://hbr.org/2015/06/a-better-way-to-map-brand-strategy

Dias, L. (2010, November 20). "Rules of Positioning." *Brand Positioning with Examples.* [Slideshare slides]. Retrieved from https://www.slideshare.net/lineldias147/brand-positioning-with-examples

Donkor, L. (2015, May 5). "Consider Cultural Differences When Marketing Global Brands." Welocalize. Retrieved from https://www.welocalize.com/consider-cultural-differences-when-marketing-global-brands/

Doyle, A. (2016, August 11). "How Companies Hire Employees." *The Balance.* Retrieved from https://www.thebalance.com/how-companies-hire-employees-2061362

D'Souza, S. (n.d.). "Why Brand Names Mean Little – And Why Personality Matters More." *Psychotactics.* Retrieved from https://www.psychotactics.com/branding-naming-a-brand/

Dunkin Donuts. (n.d.). "About Us." Retrieved from https://www.dunkindonuts.com/dunkindonuts/en/company.html

Dunn, K. (2015). "Globalization and the Consumer: What the Marketer Needs to Know." *Newmann Business Review, pgs. 16-30.* [PDF document]. Retrieved from http://www.neumann.edu/about/publications/NeumannBusinessReview/journal/Review2015/Dunn.pdf

Editor. (2014, May 30). "Why Brands Need to Understand Religion." *FCBExchange Institute of Decision Making.* Retrieved from http://fcbexchange.com/institute-of-decision-making/why-brands-need-to-understand-religion/

Elaydy, A. (2015, August 1). "There's Gaps in Market but is there a Market in Gap?" Retrieved from https://www.linkedin.com/pulse/theres-gaps-market-gap-ahmed-elaydy

Financial Accounting Standards Board. (2015, July). "Simplifying the Measurement of Inventory." *Inventory (Topic 330). 2015:11.* Retrieved from http://fasb.org/jsp/FASB/Document_C/DocumentPage?cid=1176166207669&acceptedDisclaimer=true

Fleishman, H. (2015, July 29). "13 Businesses with Brilliant Global Marketing Strategies." Retrieved from https://blog.hubspot.com/blog/tabid/6307/bid/33857/10-Businesses-We-Admire-for-Brilliant-Global-Marketing.aspx#sm.00011ocht53zdeyiya11uug6aay65

Frawley, A. (2015, March 4). "ROI Is Dead. A New Metric Is Needed for Customer Relationships: Why Brands Need to Measure Customer Experience and Engagement." *Advertising Age.* Retrieved from http://adage.com/article/digitalnext/brands-measure-experience-engagement/297426/

Friel, D. (2013, June 23). "How to Make Your Business Scalable." *Entrepreneur Handbook.* Retrieved from http://entrepreneurhandbook.co.uk/how-to-make-your-business-scalable/

GMA. (2015, June). "Retail & Consumer Insights 2015 Financial Benchmarking." [PDF document]. Retrieved from https://www.pwc.com/us/en/retail-consumer/financial-performance-report/assets/financial-performance-report.pdf

Guru Focus. (2016). "KFC (YUM!)" *Financials.* [Data File]. Retrieved from http://www.gurufocus.com/financials/YUM

Guru Focus. (2016). *McDonald's Financials.* [Data File]. Retrieved from http://www.gurufocus.com/financials/MCD

Guru Focus. (2016). "Starbucks Financials." [Data File]. Retrieved from http://www.gurufocus.com/financials/SBUX

Hardees. (n.d.). "Franchise Information." Retrieved from http://ckefranchise.com/

Harnish, V. (2010, July 22). "A Step-by-Step Process to Hiring." *Kauffman Entrepreneurs.* Retrieved from https://www.entrepreneurship.org/articles/2010/07/a-stepbystep-process-to-hiring

Heaton, J. (2011). "The Difference Between Marketing and Branding." Tronvig Group. Retrieved from http://www.tronviggroup.com/the-difference-between-marketing-and-branding/

Heeringa, V. (2015, March 5). "Is There A Market in Your Gap?" *Idealog.* 54. 116. Retrieved from http://idealog.co.nz/venture/2015/03/market-your-gap

Hofstrand, D. (n.d.). "Understanding Profitability." *Iowa State University.* Retrieved from https://www.extension.iastate.edu/AGDM/wholefarm/html/c3-24.html

Hilton. (2015). "Focused 2015 Annual Report." [PDF document]. Retrieved from http://ir.hilton.com/~/media/Files/H/Hilton-Worldwide-IR-V3/annual-report/2015-annual-report1.pdf

Hilton. (2016). "Company History." Retrieved from http://hiltonworldwide.com/

Holt, D., Quelch, J., & Taylor, E.L. (2004, September). "How Global Brands Compete." Harvard Business Review. Retrieved from https://hbr.org/2004/09/how-global-brands-compete

Housh, W. (2015, March 2). "Choosing a Business Model that will Grow with Your Company." *Entrepreneur.* Retrieved from https://www.entrepreneur.com/article/243237

Info Entrepreneurs. (n.d.). "Use Innovation to Grow Your Business." Retrieved from http://www.infoentrepreneurs.org/en/guides/use-innovation-to-grow-your-business/

Institute for Operational Excellence. (2016, May 17). "What is Operational Excellence?" Retrieved from https://instituteopex.org/site/resources/what_is_operational_excellence

Jones-Kelley, A. (2016, May). "2016 Global Best to Invest." *Site Selection Magazine.* Retrieved from http://siteselection.com/issues/2016/may/cover.cfm

Klingel, S. (2016, September). "Workshop: Best Practices in Labor Management Committees in Higher Education." *Journal of Collective Bargaining in the Academy.* Article 68. [PDF document]. Retrieved from http://thekeep.eiu.edu/cgi/viewcontent.cgi?article=1626&context=jcba

Kokemuller, N. (2016). "Advantages of Global Companies." *Houston Chronicle.* Retrieved from http://smallbusiness.chron.com/advantages-global-companies-57127.html

Lindquist, B., &Schneider, P. (November 8). "The Site Selection Process: Prepare Your Approach." *Area Development.* Retrieved from http://www.areadevelopment.com/siteSelection/nov08/site-selection-location-analysis.shtml

Lutz, A. (2015, April 7). "Nike is Going After 3 Types of Customers." *Business Insider.* Retrieval from http://www.businessinsider.com/nike-is-going-after-3-kinds-of-customers-2015-4

Marketing Donut. (2017). "Spotting Gaps in Your Market." Retrieved from http://www.marketingdonut.co.uk/market-research/spotting-gaps-in-your-market

Markgraf, B. (n.d.). "Tools for Gap Analysis." *Houston Chronicle.* Retrieved from http://smallbusiness.chron.com/tools-gap-analysis-46456.html

Maverick, J.B. (2015, February 4). "What is More Important for a Business - Profitability or Growth?" *Investopedia.* Retrieved from http://www.investopedia.com/ask/answers/020415/what-more-important-business-profitability-or-growth.asp

MBA Knowledge Base. (n.d.). "Operations Management and its Objectives." Retrieved from https://www.mbaknol.com/operations-management/operations-management-and-its-objectives/

McAllister Marketing. (2015, March 4). "The Importance of Brand Personality." Retrieved from http://mcallistermarketing.com/the-importance-of-brand-personality/

McDonald's. (2016). "Annual Report." Retrieved from http://corporate.mcdonalds.com/mcd/investors/shareholde r-information/proxy-statement-annual-report-voting-results.html

McDonald's. (2016). "Investors." Retrieved from http://corporate.mcdonalds.com/mcd/investors.html

Microsoft. (2016). "Annual Report 2016." Retrieved from https://www.microsoft.com/investor/reports/ar16/index.ht ml

MindTools. (n.d.) "PEST Analysis." Retrieved from https://www.mindtools.com/pages/article/newTMC_09.ht m

Morino, M. (2009, June 17). "Why Innovation Matters." *Stanford Social Innovation Review.* Retrieved from https://ssir.org/articles/entry/why_innovation_matters

Morningstar. (2016). "Starbucks Financials." [Data File]. Retrieved from http://financials.morningstar.com/ratios/r.html?t=SBUX

MWPVL. (2017). "The Walmart Distribution Center Network in the United States." Retrieved from http://www.mwpvl.com/html/walmart.html

Nelson, B. (2010, June 29). "Benchmark Breakdown: Key Metrics on 25 Industries." *Forbes.* [Presentation Slides]. Retrieved from https://www.forbes.com/2010/06/29/best-in-class-financial-metrics-entrepreneurs-finance-sageworks_slide.html

Northrup, L. (2016, January 22). "15 Things We Learned About the Downfall of Target Canada." *Consumerist*. Retrieved from https://consumerist.com/2016/01/22/9-things-we-learned-about-the-downfall-of-target-canada/

Old School Value. (2008, February 8). "How to Research and Determine the Growth Rate of a Company." Retrieved from https://www.oldschoolvalue.com/blog/valuation-methods/choosing-a-growth-rate/

Pappas, C. (2015, February 21). *"7 Steps to Create the Perfect Learning Unit for an eLearning Course."* Retrieved from https://elearningindustry.com/7-tips-to-create-the-perfect-learning-unit-for-an-elearning-course

Pappas, C. (2015, January 13). "6 Steps to Easily Create eLearning Courses." Retrieved from https://elearningindustry.com/easily-create-elearning-courses

Perner, L. (2017). "The Global Marketplace." *University of Southern California Marshall School of Business*. Retrieved from https://www.consumerpsychologist.com/international_marketing.html

Peterson, H. (2015, January 15). "5 Reasons Target Failed in Canada." *Business Insider*. Retrieved from http://www.businessinsider.com/why-target-canada-failed-2015-1

Princeton University. (n.d.). "Hiring Process." Retrieved from https://www.princeton.edu/hr/employment/managers/process/hireprocess/

Rains, B. (2014, May 20). "The Path to Operational Excellence Through Operational Discipline: An Ongoing Journey of Improvement." *Industry Week*. Retrieved from http://www.industryweek.com/operations/path-operational-excellence-through-operational-discipline

Rajagopal. (2007). "Brand Metrics: A Tool to Measure Performance." *Monterrey Institute of Technology and Higher Learning*. [PDF Document]. Retrieved from http://alejandria.ccm.itesm.mx/egap/documentos/2007-02-MKT.pdf

Raven, T. (2013, July 26). "Key to Operational Excellence." *Supply Chain Management Review*. Retrieved from http://www.scmr.com/article/key_to_operational_excellence

Ray Kroc. (n.d.). "Franchisopedia." Retrieved from https://franchisopedia.com/global/franchise-articles/mc_donald_s_ray_kroc/

Rizza, M. (2010, April). "Raw Material Sourcing Strategies Are Critical to Revenue and Profit Margins." *AMR Research*. [PDF document]. Retrieved from http://www.tpt.com/resources/docs/resources/amr-raw-materials-analyst-report_.pdf

Roll, M. (2015, July 8). "Five Best Practices of Global Brand Management." Insead Knowledge. [Web log content]. Retrieved from https://knowledge.insead.edu/blog/insead-blog/five-best-practices-of-global-brand-management-4136

Saed, M., & Azmi, I. (2014). "Religion and Brand Switching Behavior of Muslim Consumers." *Middle East Journal of Scientific Research*, 21(9), 1611-1617. DOI 10.5829/idosi.mejsr.2014.21.09.21737.

Schuiling, I., & Lambin, J. (n.d.). "Do Global Brands Benefit From a Unique Worldwide Image?" *Symphonya-Emerging Issues in Management*. [PDF document]. Retrieved from https://cdn.uclouvain.be/public/Exports%20reddot/iag/documents/WP_116_Schuiling.pdf

Shanmuganathan, G.D. (2014). "Influence of Cultural Factors for Global Brand Management." *Journal of Business and Management*, 3(4), 40-47.

Sheth, J., & Maholtra, N. (n.d.). "Global Consumer Culture." *Encyclopedia of International Marketing*. [PDF document]. Retrieved from http://www.uwyo.edu/sustainable/recent-research/docs/global%20consumer%20culture%20arnould.pdf

SJ. (2009, January 14). "Brand Positioning." [Slideshare slides]. Retrieved from https://www.slideshare.net/sjhus/brand-positioning-presentation

Sokolova, S. (2015, February 9). "The Importance of Creativity and Innovation in Business." Retrieved from https://www.linkedin.com/pulse/importance-creativity-innovation-business-siyana-sokolova

Staplehurst, G., & Charoenwongse, S. (n.d.). "Why Brand Personality Matters: Aligning Your Brand to Cultural Drivers of Success." *Millward Brown Point of View*. [PDF document]. Retrieved from http://www.millwardbrown.com/docs/default-source/insight-documents/points-of-view/millward_brown_pov_brand_personality.pdf

Starbucks. (2016). "Fiscal 2016 Annual Report." [PDF document]. Retrieved from http://s21.q4cdn.com/369030626/files/doc_financials/2016/Annual/FY16-Annual-Report-on-Form-10-K.pdf

Starbucks. (n.d.) "Starbucks Company International." Retrieved from https://www.starbucks.com/business/international-stores

Stark, K., and Stewart, B. (2012, July 9). "Become the Next McDonald's: 3 Steps." *INC*. Retrieved from https://www.inc.com/karl-and-bill/become-the-next-mcdonalds-3-steps.html

Statistica. (2017). "Coca-Cola's brand value from 2006 to 2017 (in billion U.S. dollars)." [Data File]. Retrieved from https://www.statista.com/statistics/326065/coca-cola-brand-value/

Statistica. (2017). "KFC Restaurants Worldwide." [Data File]. Retrieved from https://www.statista.com/statistics/256793/kfc-restaurants-worldwide-by-geographic-region/

Statistica. (2017). "List of Countries with McDonald's Restaurants." [Data File]. Retrieved from https://www.statista.com/statistics/219454/mcdonalds-restaurants-worldwide/

Statistica. (2017). "Number of Starbucks Worldwide." [Data File]. Retrieved from https://www.statista.com/statistics/266465/number-of-starbucks-stores-worldwide/

Statistica. (2017). "Target." [Data File]. Retrieved from https://www.statista.com/topics/1914/target/

Statistica. (2017). "Walmart: Total Number of Walmart Stores in the United States." [Data File]. Retrieved from https://www.statista.com/statistics/269425/total-number-of-walmart-stores-in-the-united-states-by-type/

Subway. (n.d.). "Explore Our World." Retrieved from http://www.subway.com/en-us/exploreourworld

Target. (n.d.). "Corporate Fact Sheet." Retrieved from https://corporate.target.com/press/corporate

Taussig, A. (2011, January 1). "How to Know if Your Business Will Scale." *Fortune*. Retrieved from http://fortune.com/2011/06/01/how-to-know-if-your-business-will-scale/

Tot, B. (2014, April). "Textile and Apparel Industry Report." *FPT Securities*. [PDF document]. Retrieved from http://fpts.com.vn/FileStore2/File/2014/07/01/Textile%20 and%20Apparel%20Industry%20Report%20(latest).pdf

Towse, M. (2009, March 2). "Best Practices: Creating Successful Online Modules." *Learning Solutions Magazine*. Retrieved from https://www.learningsolutionsmag.com/articles/56/best-practices-creating-successful-online-modules

U.S. General Services Administration. (n.d.). "The Site Selection Guide." [PDF document]. Retrieved from https://www.gsa.gov/graphics/pbs/GSA_Site_Selection_Gu ide_R2-sY2-i_0Z5RDZ-i34K-pR.pdf

Wahba, P. (2015, January 15). "Why Target Failed in Canada." *Fortune*. Retrieved from http://fortune.com/2015/01/15/target-canada-fail/

Walmart. (2016). "2016 Annual Report." [PDF document]. Retrieved from http://s2.q4cdn.com/056532643/files/doc_financials/2016/ annual/2016-Annual-Report-PDF.pdf

Watt, E.C. (2014, November 4). "Why Innovation Matters to Investors." *Financial Times*. Retrieved from https://www.ft.com/content/e2a7adfa-4fba-11e4-a0a4-00144feab7de

YUM Brands. (2016). "Annual Report." Retrieved from http://www.yum.com/annualreport/

YUM Brands. (2015). *KFC Development FAQs.*" Retrieved from http://www.kfcdevelopment.co.uk/faqs/

Zwilling, M. (2013, September 6). "10 Tips for Building the Most Scalable Start-Up." *Forbes.* Retrieved from https://www.forbes.com/forbes/welcome/?toURL=https:/ /www.forbes.com/sites/martinzwilling/2013/09/06/10-tips-for-building-the-most-scalable-startup/&refURL=&referrer=#799b5cce4521

Morhart, F., Malär, L., Guèvremont, A., Girardin, F., and Grohmann, B. (2015). Brand authenticity: An integrative framework and measurement scale. *Journal of Consumer Psychology*, **25**(2), 200–218. https://doi.org/10.1016/j.jcps.2014.11.00

[ii] Ries, A. and Trout, J. (2001) Positioning: The Battle for Your Mind. McGraw Hill; 1st Edition. (January 3, 2001) https://www.amazon.com/Positioning-Battle-Your-Al-Ries/dp/0071373586

[i] Levitt, T. The Globalization of Markets. *Harvard Business Review.* (May 1983) https://hbr.org/1983/05/the-globalization-of-markets

[ii] Holt, D., Quelch, J. and Taylor, E. How Global Brands Compete. *Harvard Business Review.* (September 2004) https://hbr.org/2004/09/how-global-brands-compete

[iii] Vorhauser-Smith, S. Going 'Global': How Smart Brands Adapt to Foreign Markets. *Forbes magazine.* (June 22,2012)

https://www.forbes.com/sites/sylviavorhausersmith/2012/0
6/22/cultural-homogeneity-is-not-an-automatic-by-product-
of-globalization/?sh=2334de5c5034

[iv] Gregory, L. Microsoft's Mission Statement & Vision
Statement (An Analysis). Panmore Institute. (July 20,2022)
https://panmore.com/microsoft-corporation-vision-
statement-mission-statement-
analysis#:~:text=Microsoft's%20corporate%20vision%20is%
20%E2%80%9Cto,their%20personal%20or%20organizationa
l%20development

[v] Solomon, S. THE CONTROVERSY OVER INFANT
FORMULA. *The New York Times.* (December 6, 1981)
https://www.nytimes.com/1981/12/06/magazine/the-
controversy-over-infant-formula.html?pagewanted=all

[vi] Bahri, C. Uncovering the link between religion and
economy. *India Development Review.* (October 12, 2018)
Uncovering the link between religion and economy - India
Development Review (idronline.org)

[vii] Yoder, S., Visich, J. and Rustambekov. Lessons learned
from international expansion failures and successes. Indiana
University Kelly School of Business, Business Horizons,
(2016) 59, 233-243. https://iranarze.ir/wp-
content/uploads/2016/10/E2570.pdf

End Notes

www.ingramcontent.com/pod-product-compliance
Lightning Source LLC
Chambersburg PA
CBHW020156200326
41521CB00006B/388